4

Brush Fire Wars

Brush Fire Wars

Minor Campaigns of the
British Army since 1945

by
MICHAEL DEWAR

With a foreword by
General Sir Frank Kitson,
KCB, CBE, MC, ADC (Gen)

ST. MARTIN'S PRESS
NEW YORK

ROBERT HALE LIMITED
LONDON

© *Michael Dewar 1984*
First published in Great Britain 1984

First published in the United States of America 1984
All rights reserved

Robert Hale Limited
Clerkenwell House
Clerkenwell Green
London EC1R 0HT

ISBN 0 7091 9624 5

St. Martin's Press, Inc.
175 Fifth Avenue
New York, N.Y. 10010

Library of Congress Catalog Card Number 84-40337

ISBN 0-312-10674-2

To Lavinia
My wife without whose patience
this book would not have been completed

Photoset in North Wales by
Derek Doyle & Associates, Mold, Clwyd
Printed in Great Britain by
Redwood Burn Ltd, Trowbridge, Wilts.
Bound by WBC Bookbinders Ltd

Contents

Photographs

Maps

Acknowledgements

Grateful acknowledgement is made to the following for supplying photographs: Associated Press (17); Pacemaker Press (25); Popperfoto (1, 2, 8, 9, 13, 14, 15, 20, 23, 28); Press Association (24); and Frank Spooner (27, 29). Acknowledgement is also made for permission to reproduce, or base maps upon, maps from the following publications: G. Blaxland's *The Regiments Depart*, published by William Kimber, 1970 (maps 1, 2, 3, 4, 6, 7, 8, 11, 12, 14, 16); T. Geraghty's *Who Dares Wins*, Arms and Armour Press, 1980 (22); and C. Osborne's *The Gulf States and Oman*, Croom Helm, 1977 (10).

Foreword

by

General Sir Frank Kitson, KCB, CBE, MC, ADC (Gen)

In times of peace it is easy to suppose that battles are won by the side which fields the greatest number of men, armed with the best weapons and organized in the most suitable way. To achieve this is the principal pre-occupation of those employed in the higher echelons of a country's armed forces and it is certainly very important.

But lots of men, splendidly organized and equipped, will not prevail unless they do the right thing, and this means in practice that many small groups of people, often very young people, must act with a high degree of skill, initiative, courage and determination if success is to be achieved.

Of all the armies of the Western Alliance none has afforded its officers and men so many and varied opportunities for experiencing operational conditions as the British Army. This book describes twelve campaigns spread across the thirty-eight years which elapsed following the end of World War II, and in doing so it gives the reader a chance to get the feel of some of the events which have made the British Army what it is today. The book devotes a chapter to each campaign, giving a short and simple outline of it, and for this reason alone is worth reading. But more important by far is the intimate picture which the author manages to convey of what each campaign looked like from the point of view of the small groups who did the fighting. In many cases it is obvious that he is writing about things he has seen with his own eyes, but even when this is not the case he has managed to create, from the experiences of others, impressions which are both vivid and convincing.

As one who was involved in some of the campaigns

described, I can vouch for the authenticity of these impressions. I also recommend the book for its value in helping people to understand what it feels like to be in the presence of an armed enemy, an understanding as valuable to those trying to prevent war as to those wishing to practise it.

Author's Preface

There have been many books published during the past 30 years describing one or other of the campaigns or small 'brush fire wars' in which the British Army has become involved during the post Second World War years. I have drawn on many of these for much of my information while compiling this book. (A complete list is at Appendix F.) Despite the excellence of the majority of these sources they inevitably appeal to those with a special interest in a particular corner of the world. I attempt in this book to bring these campaigns together in one volume. Inevitably the treatment of the subject matter is less comprehensive; a chapter on the Mau Mau Emergency is no substitute for an entire book. However I do aim to provide an overview of the extraordinary part played by the British Army during the retreat from Empire. It is not widely recognized that the British Army has been in action almost continuously somewhere in the world since 1945. Appendix A to this book provides an exhaustive list of every operational deployment of British troops during the period 1945-83. Clearly it is not possible to describe all these in this book. Nor do I include the Korean War (1950-53), the Anglo-French Suez Operation in November 1956 or the more recent Falklands war. These were altogether different affairs; they were conventional wars on a relatively large scale and, in the case of Korea and Suez, fought with allies outside the Commonwealth and not arising from a solely British responsibility for a dependent or protected territory. Korea, Suez and the Falklands merit individual treatment and do not fit easily in a book concerned with either counter-insurgency campaigns or small scale pre-emptive actions such as Kuwait in 1961 or Belize in 1977.

Brush Fire Wars is not an official history. It is however an accurate account of the most important brush fire wars in which British troops have been involved over the past 38 years. It is a remarkable story of military professionalism and of courage and resilience but above all of good humour and incredible patience. It is my belief that no other army could have emerged with honour from so many delicate and complex situations. With a very few exceptions the operations described in this book were carried out with the minimum force required to achieve the aim. In all cases the military machine remained subordinate to the control of its political masters. It is of interest that British troops remain involved in 1984 not only in Northern Ireland but also in Belize as a deterrent to the possibility of Guatemalan invasion, in Cyprus as part of the United Nations force deployed on the island – and of course in the Falkland Islands.

I am grateful to the many people who have taken part in the various campaigns described in this book who have shared their experiences with me. In particular I should mention Sir Guy Campbell, Major-General John Watts, Major-General John Akehurst, Lieutenant-Colonel Malcolm Dewar, Lieutenant-Colonel Roger Wheeler, Lieutenant-Colonel Peter Treneer-Michel, Major Dare Newell and Mr Tom Fitch. I am also most grateful to the invaluable help provided by the staffs of the Ministry of Defence Library in Whitehall, the Royal United Services Institute Library, the Prince Consort's Library in Aldershot and the Royal Military Academy Library at Sandhurst. I am also grateful to Michael Jordan for typing the entire manuscript for me.

I draw on my own experiences in Cyprus, Borneo and Northern Ireland and to a lesser extent in Malaya for much of the material in the chapters describing these particular campaigns.

I have written *Brush Fire Wars* with the intention of reaching a wider readership than is usually realized by the conventional work of military history. If I have succeeded in creating a greater awareness of the unique part played in post-war world history by the British Army I will be well satisfied.

M.D.

1

The British Army in 1945

In 1945 the British Army found itself in occupation of a larger part of the world than ever before. Not only were British troops stationed throughout the Empire as it then was but also, as a result of the defeat of Germany and Japan, in many other parts of the world too. Part of the Eighth Army, having fought its way up the Italian Peninsula, now occupied that part of Austria allotted to them. Meanwhile Field Marshal Montgomery's 21st Army Group settled into what was to become the British Zone of Germany. Three divisions of British troops were dispatched to Greece to support the Greek Royalists in their struggle to crush the Communist guerillas who had controlled most of the country since 1944. In North Africa token forces occupied the Italians' East African possessions in Abyssinia, Eritrea and Somaliland. As well as the British troops in Egypt and Palestine, it had been necessary to enter Syria, Iraq and Persia. In the Far East as well as repossessing the British colonies of Burma, Malaya, Singapore, Borneo and Hong Kong, the British Army was required, in the absence of a Dutch army, to take over the administration of the Dutch East Indies. The Indonesian nationalist leader, Doctor Sukarno, had with the backing of the Japanese set up a republic. It took nearly three divisions of British and Indian Army troops to subdue the rebels and it was not until 1946 that Dutch troops arrived to relieve them.

The vacuum left by the surrender of Japan also had to be filled in Siam and French Indo-China. The French Army was not able to assume control completely in Indo-China until early 1946 by which time British troops had become embroiled with the nationalist forces of Ho Chi Minh.

Thus a vast army of three million men found itself scattered across the face of the globe. This army had been raised to fight the powerful Axis war machine. Clearly it would soon be redundant, or so everyone thought. One thing was certain however; the army would have to be drastically reduced in size. Regular regiments were axed and those that remained were reduced to a single battalion each. There were some exceptions to this rule, notably among the Foot Guards who managed to keep ten battalions. There were though some newcomers to join the older regiments: the Parachute Regiment, which had been formed in 1942 and which had grown to seventeen battalions by 1945, was slashed to three battalions and one independent company by 1947. Eight battalions of Gurkhas were formed from the Gurkha regiments of the Indian Army. During the months leading up to partition in India and subsequent independence the Indian Army Gurkha regiments were given the option of either remaining servants of the British Crown or joining the newly independent Indian Army Gurkhas. Though most opted to join the Indian Army it was perhaps fortunate for Britain that it was possible to form a Brigade of Gurkhas within the post-war British Army. The contribution of the diminutive Gurkhas from the hills of Nepal to British military success since 1945 has been out of all proportion to their limited numbers. Though under the control of the Admiralty, the third addition to the ranks of the infantry in the immediate post-war period were the Royal Marine Commandos. The Commandos had been raised by Churchill in 1940, originally under army control, to carry out harassing raids on occupied Europe.

Thus immediately after the war there remained seventy-seven infantry battalions not including the Gurkhas or, of course, the three Royal Marine Commandos. The Royal Armoured Corps consisted of some thirty regiments, the Royal Artillery of some sixty-nine regiments, and the Royal Engineers of twenty-three regiments. The total planned strength of the post-war National Service Army was some 305,000 but in fact this figure had been increased by nearly 100,000 by 1951 due in part to the Korean War. Such was the shape of the army with which Britain faced the post-war world. Though vastly reduced from the three million men under arms at the end of the war, it was still by British standards a large standing army. Today, after the withdrawal from Empire, the British Army is a mere 135,000 strong, of which 55,000 are stationed on the mainland of Europe and committed to the NATO alliance.

The post-war army was of course a National Service Army. In July 1947 Prime Minister Attlee steered the National Service Act through Parliament. The Act came into effect on 1st January 1949 from which date conscripts would be bound to serve for one year with the colours and for six on the reserve. The commitment to the colours was very soon increased to eighteen months and then further increased to two years in the Defence White Paper of 31st August 1950. National Service continued until Duncan Sandys, Defence Minister in the Macmillan Government, announced on 5th April 1957 that National Service would be progressively reduced up until 1960, after which no more conscripts would be called up. By 1st January 1963 the British Army was once again an all-regular force.

Leaving aside Korea, Suez and the Falklands, the campaigns which the Army fought during the 1945-83 period were almost all counter-insurgency in nature. Of all the former colonial powers the British experience in counter-insurgency is probably the richest. The Dutch in Indonesia, the French in Algeria and Indo-China, and the Portuguese in Angola and Mozambique all carried out counter-insurgency operations in their colonies. Even Hitler's Wehrmacht was involved in what can properly be called counter-insurgency operations in Russia and Yugoslavia. The United States was similarly involved in the Philippines from 1896 and in Haiti 1916-34. The British experience, however, has been gained over a long period of time during which an Empire has been established, held and lost; it falls into three main phases: the century between the accession of Queen Victoria to the throne in 1837 and the outbreak of World War II in 1939, the Second World War itself (1939-45) and the post-war period. In each of these periods the army acquired experience that enabled it to survive subsequent threats. In the period of Queen Victoria's rule (to 1901) the British fought over forty-five small colonial wars; typical of the period were the Indian Mutiny, the campaign against the Mahdi in the Sudan when Gordon was killed, the Zulu Wars in South Africa, disagreements with the Egyptians, clashes with various war lords in China, and finally the Boer War in South Africa, the latter being very much a war against rural guerillas. In the 1920s both the army and the newly formed RAF were required to deal with dissident tribesmen in Iraq, Somalia, the North-West Frontier and the Aden Protectorates.

During the Second World War, although the army's enemies were essentially conventional in nature and habit, there were several opportunities for perfecting counter-insurgency techniques. In the war against Japan in Burma the army developed techniques of jungle warfare that were later codified and taught at the Jungle Warfare School at Kota Tingi near Jahore Bahru in Malaya. From 1943 Communist guerillas fighting the Japanese in the jungles of Malaya were aided by a British force known as Force 136 who were infiltrated by boat into Japanese-held territory and themselves fought very much in the fashion of guerillas. The Long Range Desert Group formed to operate behind the lines in North Africa were the forerunners of the SAS who inherited many of their techniques. Also the partisans in Yugoslavia fighting the Germans were advised and helped by British officers. Even the exploits of the Special Operations Executive (SOE) in France provided direct experience of guerilla operations for many of its operatives who had been recruited from the army.

Thus by 1945 the British Army was already well versed in techniques suitable for small operations and minor campaigns – or as they have since been dubbed 'Brush Fire Wars'. This was just as well because from the moment that the British Army became embroiled in Palestine it was to be committed without a respite for the next thirty-eight years in a series of conflicts; British troops are still deployed today in Northern Ireland, Belize, Cyprus, the Falklands, and, in an advisory capacity, in Dhofar and Zimbabwe.

Palestine had been brewing since before the Second World War. When Germany was defeated, the storm broke.

2

Palestine
1945-48

On 14th May 1948 at half past eleven at night a British naval flotilla moved slowly out of Haifa Bay on the coast of Israel. A screen of destroyers and frigates surrounded the flagship, the aircraft carrier HMS *Ocean*, and the cruiser HMS *Euryalus*. On board *Euryalus* was the British High Commissioner to Palestine, Sir Alan Cunningham. At midnight, when the ships reached the limit of Palestine's territorial waters, the High Commissioner turned to salute the flagship. At the same instant the State of Israel was born. It was the 6th of Iyar in the Jewish Calendar of the year 5708.

The League of Nations had entrusted Britain with the Mandate for Palestine in 1917 after the British Army with the help of indigenous Arabs had ejected the Turks from the country. The League supported the British proposal, which had been first stated in the Balfour Declaration of November 1917, to establish in Palestine 'a National Home for the Jews'. Palestine at that time contained approximately 600,000 Arabs and only 55,000 Jews. Not surprisingly the Arabs felt that the League of Nations and more particularly their agents, the British, had got their priorities confused. As Jewish immigration into Palestine gained momentum the Arabs were driven to rebellion. By 1939 this rebellion had been put down but it took seventeen British battalions to do it. Though militarily defeated the Arabs succeeded in forcing the British in their contentious White Paper of March 1939 into restricting Jewish immigration to 75,000 over the next five years and no more after that without the agreement of the Arabs. It was now the

Jews that had a grievance.

When the European war broke out most Jews co-operated with the British war effort – all in fact except the notorious Stern gang. Abraham Stern, a Polish Jew, came to Palestine in 1940. He broke with the Irgun – at that time the most extreme of the Jewish para-military groups in Palestine – and formed the Lehi or Freedom Fighters of Israel movement. His policy was to reach an accommodation with Hitler to move all Jews living in Europe to designated areas of Palestine in return for assisting Germany to gain the entire country. He felt that there was a greater chance of independence for the State of Israel by this means than under British rule. To this end he instigated a series of guerilla attacks against the police and the army. However in February 1942 the police caught up with Stern who was killed in the exchange of fire that ensued. Anti-British feeling was maintained by the arrival later in 1942 of Menahem Begin, one of Stern's original followers in Poland; he was appointed Commander of the Irgun in 1943 and in 1944 announced the launching of a revolt against British rule. He cut all ties with the more moderate Haganah, a legal people's army sanctioned by the British Administration since the earliest days of the mandate to act as a home guard to protect Jewish settlements against Arab attack. He agreed that as long as the British Army was fighting Hitler they would not be a target for the Irgun. At that time, despite a series of bombing attacks against British police stations between May and September 1944 and in contrast to the Lehi, Begin sought to avoid personal injury.

A new slant was put on the Palestinian problem in November 1944 when Lord Moyne, a British Minister of State in Egypt, was assassinated by two Lehi agents in Cairo. The Jewish Agency under the leadership of David Ben Gurion publicly condemned both the Lehi and the Irgun. In a subsequent operation organized by the Jewish Agency, the Haganah detained the entire Irgun High Command with the notable exception of Begin who managed to evade capture along with one aide. But the success was an illusory one: new enthusiasts flocked to join the Irgun on the conclusion of the war in Europe in May 1945. By the end of that year the Haganah had formed a working relationship with the Irgun and the Lehi, both of which had been little more than a

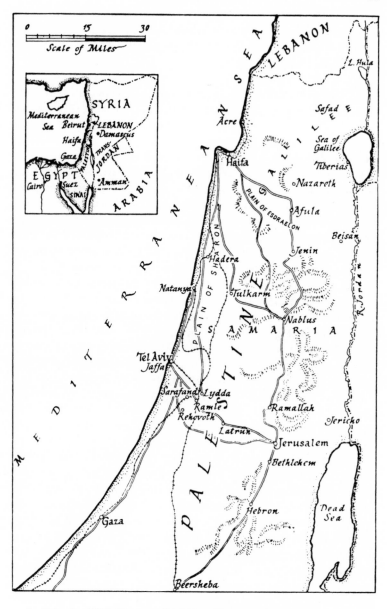

1   Palestine 1945-48: area of British military involvement

military nuisance to the British, but now that organized Palestinian Jewry in the form of the Agency had joined the fray a much more serious long-term threat to the British position in the Middle East existed.

In September 1945 there were a great many British troops in Palestine, not so much as a result of the threat to the internal security of the country but more as a result of their role as Middle East Strategic Reserve. Both the 1st Infantry Division and the 6th Airborne Division arrived during the course of 1945. The 6th Airborne arrived just in time for the beginning of the Jewish offensive on the night of 31st October. The bombing offensive was aimed primarily at the railway system, but police vehicles and the Haifa oil refinery were also targets. Though it had not been the intention to kill anyone in these attacks one soldier, one policeman and two railway workers lost their lives. The attacks of 31st October were timed to influence the statement on future British policy in Palestine which Ernest Bevin, the Foreign Secretary, was known to be about to make. On 13th November Bevin announced that the 1939 White Paper would be revoked and that Jewish immigration would be permitted to continue at the rate of 1500 a year. This of course was a fraction of the requirement and was a compromise that would satisfy nobody. However it was also announced that an Anglo-American Committee would be convened to find a more lasting solution. The package, needless to say, displeased the Jews. On 14th November there was serious rioting in Jerusalem and Tel Aviv. At nightfall the first of many post-war decisions by British colonial administrations to call in troops in aid of the civil power was taken. The police, no longer able to contain the situation in Tel Aviv on their own, were reinforced by soldiers of the 8th Parachute Battalion. Order was restored but only after some shots were fired causing one fatal casualty among the crowd. Rioting broke out again the following day and continued until the 20th. Several more airborne battalions were deployed to contain the situation. Their efforts were successful and the riots in Tel Aviv subsided.

This had been the first of many similar incidents that were to occur with monotonous regularity in various parts of the world during the British withdrawal from Empire. The Army employed what became traditional tactics of crowd dispersal that lasted until the violence of Northern Ireland, nearly thirty years later, made them redundant. Troops advanced towards a crowd in 'box' formation and displayed a banner proclaiming 'Disperse or we fire'. The message was reinforced by loudhailer over which magistrates were required to issue dire warnings of legal retribution. In the last resort single shots were fired at selected ringleaders which usually had the desired effect of dispersing the crowd fairly rapidly.

Later in November British troops met further resistance from Jewish villagers whose houses were being searched for illegal arms or whose occupants were being screened for intelligence purposes. In the ensuing violence six Jews were killed. The situation was clearly worsening. More troops were rushed to Palestine from Germany.

Early in the New Year during February the Jews struck successfully at three RAF airfields destroying several aircraft. Their campaign continued into April when they made further attacks upon the railway system. However it did not always go the way of the Irgun. After one attack on the railways, troops of the 8th Battalion the Parachute Regiment succeeded in ambushing an Irgun patrol killing some of its members and forcing the remainder to surrender. Possibly in retaliation for this British Army success the Lehi escalated their campaign of violence against the army on 25th April. In a cowardly attack against soldiers of the 5th Battalion the Parachute Regiment they murdered seven soldiers seated in a tent on the Tel Aviv waterfront quite unaware of the danger they were in. On 18th June the Irgun kidnapped five unarmed British officers in an attempt to head off the execution of two Irgun men sentenced to death for their part in a raid on a British military base some three months previously in which a Jewish policeman had been shot dead and others wounded. Although three of the hostages were released, the Jews announced that the fate of the remaining two depended on the death sentence on the two Irgun men being carried out or not. It will never be known for sure if the new General Officer Commanding, Lieutenant-General Sir Evelyn Barker, was unduly influenced by this threat. In any event he commuted the death sentences to life imprisonment and the two officers were released. This affair had been the last straw for the British military authorities; in consequence they planned a vast operation involving all British military units in Palestine to search and screen suspect Jewish houses and their inhabitants. This included members of the Jewish Agency. Operation Agatha, as it was called, met with considerable success: in all some 600 weapons were captured. The Irgun, not to be outdone, pulled off their most outrageous coup yet. On 22nd July they planted large quantities of explosive under the King David Hotel which was used for government and military offices. Despite a telephoned warning of an impending explosion and a gun battle that had resulted from the terrorists being surprised in the act of planting the explosive, most of the occupants of the offices were not warned. In the ensuing explosion over ninety people were killed.

A four-day cordon and search operation of Tel Aviv followed involving 17,000 British troops. More arms were discovered and hundreds of suspects detained. Once again the elusive Menahem Begin escaped detection. By this stage even the moderate Jewish Agency had determined that their only choice was to work for the removal of British rule. There had been one last chance of compromise the previous April when the Anglo-American Committee of Inquiry recommended that 100,000 Jewish refugees be transferred from Europe to Palestine. The British announced that they would agree to the plan but only if both Arabs and Jews surrendered all their weapons. There was, of course, no chance of either side complying. By July 1946 27,000 British troops were involved in Palestine. Only one year after peace in Europe, a vast British Army was again in action – but this time they were engaged in an impossible task which none of them relished. Although there were occasional incidents of indiscipline, the behaviour of the troops under conditions of extreme provocation was remarkably restrained. During 1946 forty-nine British soldiers had been killed and many more wounded. But worse was to come in 1947. In February that year Ernest Bevin, at a loss what to do with two intractable adversaries, washed his hands of the affair and referred the matter to the United Nations.

In the meantime the violence dragged on. On 16th April four Irgun terrorists were hanged in Acre Prison for serious crimes of violence against the army. On 4th May the Irgun retaliated by blowing a hole in the wall of Acre Prison enabling a large proportion of the prisoners held there to escape. The perpetrators of this audacious act were shot or captured by two British privates who took it upon themselves to give chase in a commandeered car.

Eventually in June the United Nations fact-finding commission arrived in Palestine. Whether by coincidence or design a perfect propaganda opportunity for the Jews arose only three weeks after the arrival of the Commission. Ever since 1940 the Royal Navy had intercepted ships carrying Jews to Palestine and escorted the refugees on board to internment camps on the island of Cyprus. In support of the policy of annual quotas of immigration into Palestine forty-seven ships were intercepted between 1940 and 1948 and 65,307 Jews interned. There is no suggestion, except by the most extreme anti-British Jews, that these camps were run in any other manner than properly and humanely. However in July 1947 one such ship carrying German Jewish refugees was not permitted to land its human cargo in Cyprus. Bevin, in an attempt to stem the tide, ordered that the 4,000 German Jews on board the *Exodus* should be deported to their port of embarkation in the south of France. They refused to disembark in France and so were escorted back to Hamburg to their country of origin. As the refugees were dragged ashore in Hamburg almost every newspaper in the world reported the story with incredulous horror. Whatever Bevin's motives it was undoubtedly a monumental public relations gaffe. Only the British troops who had the unenviable task of escorting the unfortunate refugees back to Hamburg emerged with any sort of honour. Though constantly provoked in order to provide evidence of 'British brutality' their behaviour was impeccable throughout the whole unfortunate affair. The young National Servicemen did their duty with as much kindness and understanding as was possible in the circumstances.

Finally in November 1947 the UN decided on partition for Palestine. During the period between the visit of the Commission in June and the announcement of their decision in November the Irgun had taken more British hostages as bargaining counters for three of their members under sentence of death. On 29th July the three Jews were executed. On 31st July the bodies of the two British hostages, sergeants in Intelligence, were found hanging from a tree. There was some evidence in the weeks following this incident of 'reprisals' by British troops. Clearly a political solution was desperately needed. The news of partition was met among most British soldiers with a feeling of relief. Although the Jews amounted to approximately one third of the population of Palestine, the UN decision gave them half the country. The Arab population registered their disapproval by attacking Jews and Jewish property whenever and wherever the opportunity presented itself. The Jews responded with even greater violence. For the first of many occasions the British soldiers found themselves in the middle. The UN announcement on partition was followed swiftly by a British Government announcement that the Mandate would end on 15th May 1948 though some British troops would remain until 1st August to protect the dismantling of vital military installations and to ensure an orderly withdrawal.

Christmas Day 1947 was a dreadful affair. In clashes throughout Palestine, mostly instigated by disaffected Arabs, more than a hundred Arabs and Jews were killed. The Irgun struck back immediately by taking the village of Deri Yassim and killing 254 men, women and children; 6,000 Arabs fled from Tiberias and another 40,000 from Haifa. Herein lay the seeds of the Palestinian refugee problem which is no nearer being solved thirty-six years later. By the spring of 1948 no effective central government control existed over most of Palestine. Armed Arab gangs roamed over much of Galilee while the Haganah controlled most of the ground further south. The army by this stage had largely opted out though even the problem of withdrawal, which was the main priority, was not without its attendant dangers. On 20th February a terrorist mine wrecked a train carrying military equipment to Egypt killing twenty-eight soldiers and wounding another thirty-five. A week later a raid by the Irgun on a British Army camp near Latrun claimed at least another five lives and succeeded in its purpose of removing large quantities of rifles and ammunition. This raid and many others like it was successful largely because the raiders arrived at the camp gates in British Army vehicles and uniforms. They had accumulated these over the years; some had been issued during the war to Jews involved in the British war effort but most had been stolen in raids or removed from captured servicemen. Disguised raiding parties added another dimension of complexity to the already difficult task of British soldiers in Palestine.

British forces now occupied enclaves around Jerusalem, Jaffa, and Haifa. In the north two platoons of Irish Guards supported by a troop of the 17/21st Lancers and some policemen made a fighting withdrawal on 16th April from their position in the small town of Safad in the extreme north-east corner of Galilee. The town had been entirely surrounded by Arab invaders from across the border. A similar withdrawal was made from Tiberias on 28th April. There was little doubt that by this stage the army was a little tired of being the only military force in the world that was still being shot at two years after the end of the war. What was worse was that they were being shot at by both sides. Moreover there was little enthusiasm for the fight among the general public at home. The Government plan was now quite simply to get out as quickly and painlessly as possible. There was a barely disguised hope that the Arab Legion in Jordan commanded by General Glubb Pasha, a British soldier of some distinction, would sweep into Palestine forcing the Jews to scream for British help.

Even Britain's wartime allies were exasperated by the British attitude. President Truman said at the time 'the Jews are so emotional and the Arabs so difficult to talk with that it is impossible to get anything done. The British of course, have been exceedingly non-co-operative'.

By the end of April the military situation was approaching conventional warfare. In Jerusalem the Jews seized a house belonging to a prominent Arab doctor. When the Jews refused to move the Highland Light Infantry were ordered to remove them by force. They were supported by a troop of Cromwell tanks manned by men of the 4th/7th Dragoon Guards and some armoured cars belonging to the Life Guards. They also had artillery and machine-gun support. Needless to say the assault was successful and a large number of Jewish fighters were killed or captured. At the same time the Irgun were removed forcibly from the foothold they had gained in Jaffa. Again the guns of the Royal Artillery, in this case the 41st Field Regiment, played a vital role in persuading the Jews that it was not worth taking the British Army on in open warfare. In order to secure the final British withdrawal reinforcements were

dispatched to Palestine on 1st May. They consisted of two
Royal Marine Commandos from Malta, one infantry battalion
from Cyprus and the 4th Royal Tank Regiment from Egypt.
The reinforcements proved unnecessary as, in the event, there
was no more anti-British violence of any consequence during
the remaining two weeks before the departure of the High
Commissioner. On 14th May Sir Alan Cunningham left
Jerusalem for the port of Haifa where he boarded HMS
Euryalus. When the Mandate expired at midnight on 14th May
the Government of Palestine was transferred to the care of a
United Nations Commissioner. It was thirty years and five
months since General Allenby's Army had first entered the
Jaffa Gate.

After the departure of the High Commissioner half the
troops remaining in Palestine headed south and thence into
Egypt passing elements of the Egyptian Army going in the
opposite direction on their way to invade Israel. Meanwhile in
the north those troops entrusted with the task of the defence of
the port of Haifa withdrew into the enclave surrounding the
port. Haifa was commanded by Lieutenant-General
MacMillan, GOC British troops Palestine and Trans Jordan,
for the next six weeks while the business of removing military
hardware went ahead surprisingly uneventfully. He was the last
British soldier to leave Palestine on 30th June.

During the three-year post-war campaign in Palestine
twenty British officers and 203 soldiers were killed. Many more
were wounded. It had not been a glamorous nor a glorious
campaign despite many individual acts of gallantry. The army
was well out of it. Nevertheless, despite appallingly complex
circumstances, the regiments acquitted themselves well. Little
did they realize that this much and more was to be asked of
them again and again over the ensuing thirty-five years.

3

Malaya
1948-60

Arthur Walker managed the Elphin Estate rubber plantation in Sungei Siput some eighteen miles north of Ipoh in North Malaya. Shortly after he had started work in his office on the morning of 16th June 1948 three young Chinese rode up to the estate offices on bicycles. They knocked on his door, bade him good morning and then shot him twice through the chest. The same day two other European estate managers were killed in the Sungei Siput area. A State of Emergency was proclaimed that evening in several districts in Perak and Johore. This was extended to the whole of the two States on the following day and on 18th June a State of Emergency was proclaimed for the whole of Malaya. So began the twelve-year-long anti-Communist war in Malaya.

The Malayan Communist Party had been formed in 1930. When Russia suddenly became an ally of Great Britain in 1941 the Malay Communist Party was instructed to give all possible help to the British against the Japanese including the waging of guerilla warfare in the rear of the Japanese armies. As it became increasingly apparent that Singapore would fall the British agreed to train and equip 'stay-behind parties' of Communist guerillas. Before Singapore fell they succeeded in training 200 men who set up camps in the jungle. This force, which became known as the Malayan People's Anti-Japanese Army, was by 1945 7,000 strong. It consisted mostly of Communist Party members, though some were simply anti-Japanese. From 1943 the guerillas were joined by the men of Force 136, which eventually reached a strength of some forty

2   Malaya: focus of British operations 1948-60

officers and about 250 other ranks including a large proportion of radio operators. Force 136 organized the delivery of arms, ammunition, equipment and supplies by submarine and parachute and also acted as a liaison group between the Communist leadership and the Allied Commander-in-Chief, Lord Louis Mountbatten, in preparing the guerillas to act in support of the intended British landings on the coast of Malaya. In the event, of course, these landings never took place since the Japanese surrendered after Hiroshima.

The Malayan People's Anti-Japanese Army (MPAJA) was disbanded on 1st December 1945. Each man received a bounty of £45 and was required to hand in his personal weapon to the authorities. Many did but some 4,000 took their weapons, mainly Japanese, into hiding.

Malaya in 1945 had a population of about five million of whom 49 per cent were Malays, 38 per cent Chinese and 12 per cent Indians. The remaining one per cent consisted mostly of the indigenous Aborigines and of Europeans. The easy-going and uncompetitive Malays, who are thought to have migrated originally from the continental north, were and still are very different in character from the two million industrious Chinese, most of whom were born in Malaya but who were in reality aliens whose loyalties were rooted in China, a country which they had never seen but from which they had brought their women, religion and customs. Every city and almost every village in Malaya had its Chinatown – hectic, hardworking and rich. But 600,000 of the Chinese in Malaya belonged to a different category. These were the squatters, many of whom had fled the cities during the Japanese occupation to try and eke out a living in ramshackle home-made huts on the jungle fringe as far removed from the Japanese as possible. They worked land to which they had no title and survived by raising pigs, ducks and chickens and growing vegetables.

Lastly there were the British who had first come to Malaya when Captain Francis Light of the East India Company started trading in Penang in 1785. Raffles founded the port of Singapore in 1819. By 1874 both Malaya and Singapore were in effect British colonies though the Sultans always retained certain rights and privileges, mostly in matters of local government. However it was not until 1909 that the remaining

States of Perlis, Kedah, Kelantan and Trengganu were ceded to
Britain by Siam.

In 1948 the Malays, the Chinese, the Indians, the Aborigines
and the British all lived in one of the wildest but most beautiful
countries on earth. Malaya is also a guerilla's paradise. All but
small areas of coastal plain are covered in thick jungle. In
places the jungle stretches for miles, at sea level often
becoming mangrove swamp. The spine of the country is a
7,000-foot-high mountain range running north–south and
covered in primary jungle. The canopy formed by the foliage
of the 200-foot-high jungle trees keeps the jungle floor
relatively clear of undergrowth. In more accessible regions that
had been cultivated at some stage either by the Aborigines or
by Chinese squatters the undergrowth had often taken over
again forming impenetrable 'secondary' jungle where the sun
had encouraged a thick and prickly growth.

On the jungle edge life revolved around the villages or
kampongs usually situated by a river or coastal inlet. Palms
produced oil, roofing and coconuts; paddy fields produced the
staple diet of the Malays, Chinese and Indians. An amazing
variety of tropical fruits flourished and fish abounded in the
sea and rivers.

Against this background was fought one of the most vicious
and protracted wars in which the British Army has ever taken
part. It was moreover a war in which the Communist Chinese
were led by the same capable and resolute men who had fought
alongside the British from 1942 to 1945.

The bulk of the British garrison in Malaya in June 1948 was
provided by the Brigade of Gurkhas who had six battalions
stationed on the mainland. A seventh battalion was stationed
on Singapore Island. There were also three British Infantry
battalions and a Gunner regiment stationed either in
Singapore or Penang. The General Officer Commanding
Malaya District was a Major-General Boucher, an ex-Gurkha
himself.

The Malayan Police Force had a regular strength of only
10,000. Its morale was low and its equipment second rate. The
immediate aim therefore was to instil sufficient confidence into
the police force to free soldiers for offensive action in the
jungle. Taking into account those men needed for

administrative duties, the British and Gurkha battalions could put about 4,000 riflemen into the jungle in 1948. The effective strength of the MPAJA, now reconstituted in the jungle as the Malayan People's Anti-British Army (MPABA), was almost exactly the same. Because initially there were insufficient police a large number of soldiers were tied down in static guards and escort duties. More encouraging was the response of the civilian population, particularly the British rubber planters, to the terrorist threat. Home Guard units proved to be a highly effective way of discouraging attacks on isolated rubber estates, and recruiting for the Special Constabulary, the Malay Regiment and the Auxiliary Police improved dramatically.

The basis of the campaign against the terrorists was the Emergency Regulations passed by the Federal Legislature in June 1948, revised in 1949 and amended in 1953. The most important measure in these regulations was the requirement for the entire population over twelve years old to register at police stations and to have their photograph and thumbprint recorded on an identity card. No identity card system will work unless the holder has a real incentive to look after his card. This was achieved in Malaya by making the identity card a passport to obtain food, certain grants, the right to live in a resettled village and some other advantages. Despite attempts by the guerillas to disrupt the system by destroying identity cards – this was overcome by issuing tallies in return for ID cards – the system proved highly effective in preventing guerillas moving about freely on the roads and rubber estates. It also made it virtually impossible for the guerillas to live among the people in the villages. If such a state of affairs can be maintained for any length of time then perhaps the most important requisite for defeating a guerilla insurgency is achieved.

The second main provision of the Emergency Regulations was the power to arrest and detain without trial – the notorious Regulation 17D. Although such a step goes against the basic precepts of a democratic state it was considered to be a necessary evil in the battle against a ruthless and organized guerilla enemy. Communist techniques of intimidation were particularly effective and few witnesses were prepared to give evidence in open court. In these circumstances the police, who often had hard evidence against guerillas, were able to act, despite the reluctance of witnesses to give evidence, against guerillas.

The power to impose curfews was deemed to be another necessary restriction of individual liberty. The curfew was used sparingly and in various forms. Blanket curfews would have caused widespread resentment. Therefore they were used as a form of collective punishment in areas where the population was persistently supporting the guerillas.

Another emergency power was the right to search private property without a warrant. This was often a distasteful task but paid dividends in terms, of gathering intelligence and preventing food and supplies being stored for the guerillas in the jungle. If anyone was caught with an unauthorized weapon it was mandatory for judges to impose the death sentence though the sentence could be commuted, particularly in return for information. Similarly anyone found with Communist propaganda or documents was liable to imprisonment for up to ten years. These regulations were enforced from the beginning of the Emergency, though certain late additions were made in 1953. However the Emergency Regulations that were passed in June 1948 achieved their main aim which was to separate the guerilla from the people by forcing him into the jungle. By the time the Communist Party was proscribed in July 1948 Chin Peng had recalled his Communist Army to the jungle. His plan was a classic Communist one, namely to 'liberate' the country in logical steps working outwards from his jungle base. The first stage would be to gain control over the rubber estates on the jungle fringe, then to extend his control to the neighbouring kampongs until he was in a position to establish a 'Peoples Republic' from which he could recruit his guerilla army to take on the British and Malayan Armies in open warfare as subsequently happened in Vietnam. Chin Peng organized his guerillas into two basic components, namely the 4,000–5,000 members of the Malayan People's Anti-British Army, who were the uniformed strike force of the Communist movement, and the Min Yuen or Masses Movement which consisted ostensibly of innocent citizens in every walk of life whose task it was to support the guerilla army in the jungle. The guerilla army in the jungle was further divided into fighting units and Malayan Communist Party (MCP) branches. The role of the

MCP branches was to be the point of contact between fighting units and the Min Yuen.

By April 1949 the Emergency Regulations began to take effect and there was a marked fall in the number of guerilla incidents. In an attempt to win wider support for their cause the MPABA was renamed the Malayan Races' Liberation Army (MRLA). For his part Sir Henry Gurney, who had been sworn in as High Commissioner in Kuala Lumpur in October 1948, lost no time in implementing the Emergency Regulations, some of which had been initiated before his arrival and some of which he introduced. Meanwhile the total number of fighting units available to the authorities had risen from the June 1948 figure of eleven major units to seventeen – nine British, six Gurkha and two Malay, of which only one was stationed in Singapore.

In October 1949, after a slight lull in the war, there was a sudden resurgence of violence. The targets were in the main village police posts. Kampongs could only be 'liberated' if village police posts were eliminated. However, despite successful attacks on some police stations, the police force as a whole remained loyal. This was due in large part to the effective system that was developed for reinforcing police stations under attack. Infantry battalions were spread out in company-sized camps so that they were never too far away from any police station. In response to a telephone call or even a telephone line going dead a quick reaction force would be dispatched to the police station under attack. Thus it was that these vital police stations were established and maintained.

Although the army had a number of successful contacts in the jungle throughout 1949 the situation was on the whole a depressing one. By March 1950 the total number killed by the Communist terrorists since the beginning of the Emergency was estimated to be approximately 850 civilians, 325 policemen and 150 soldiers. Admittedly the security forces claimed to have killed over 1,000 terrorists and captured another 650. Some 350 had also surrendered over the same period. But the strength of the MRLA in the jungle remained approximately the same due to a steady flow of replacements recruited by the Min Yuen. It is no exaggeration to say that in March 1950 the security forces were losing the war. The guerillas were by now killing a hundred civilians a month and were still operating in groups of a hundred or more. The main reason for this seeming invulnerability was that, despite the provisions of the Emergency Regulations, the guerillas were still getting all the logistic support they required from the squatters on the jungle fringe. Among those who suffered most during this frightening period were the planters. One such man was Peter Lucy who, with his wife Jenny and two young children, lived in a bungalow on their plantation only seven miles from Kuala Lumpur. During one two-week period in 1951 there were twenty-five terrorist attacks on the Lucys' home. On one night there were three. Peter Lucy and his two special constables normally took up fire positions outside the bungalow and returned the terrorists' fire. Jenny, wishing to be near her children in moments of danger, manned a bren gun at the nursery window. As she opened fire at terrorists on the jungle fringe she kept an eye on her twins. The remarkable sight of this extremely beautiful and elegant woman prone behind a bren gun caught the imagination of everyone who knew the Lucys and typified the determination of the planters not to be intimidated.

It became increasingly clear that a change of direction was required. This was provided by Lt-General Sir Harold Briggs who arrived in Kuala Lumpur on 5th April 1950 to take up the new appointment of Director of Operations. He was given the executive power by Sir Henry Gurney to co-ordinate the army, police and air force and any other agency supporting them. He quickly appreciated that, if the war was to be won, it was necessary to deprive the enemy of their system of supply and communications. He decided that the only way to achieve this was to resettle the 423,000 Chinese squatters into New Villages. But his aim was not only to resettle the squatters but also to improve their standard of living. This, he calculated, would make supporting the Government a more attractive proposition and so increase the flow of intelligence. He also set up a system of Committees from the War Council at central government level through Briggs' own Operations Committee to War Executive Committees at State and District Levels (SWECS and DWECS). These committees involved civil government, police and military in close co-operation. Home Guard representatives and even community leaders were co-opted to provide advice on local affairs. The committee system provided the impetus needed to plan and build the 410 New Villages that were needed to resettle the squatters. This programme was achieved within two years of the inception of what became known as the Briggs Plan. It was also in 1951 in June that General Briggs put into effect 'operation starvation' which aimed to deprive the MLRA of its sources of food.

On 6th October 1951 the guerillas successfully ambushed and killed Sir Henry Gurney, the High Commissioner, while he was motoring northwards with his wife for a holiday at Fraser's Hill. This terrible blow followed four months of intense enemy activity during which the guerillas had reacted angrily to the New Villages, often spraying them with machine-gun fire from the jungle. But, although things seemed to be going their way, their losses during 1951 had increased dramatically as the army learned to locate their camps in the jungle. There were now twenty-six fighting units in Malaya, fourteen British, eight Gurkha and four Malay. These troops included 22 SAS who had developed the technique of landing by parachute on the jungle canopy and remaining in the jungle for at least fourteen days providing vital intelligence on the location of enemy camps.

In order to survive the guerillas were forced to cease operating in regiments and companies and to split up into platoon-sized groups. Attacks by up to 200 armed men on police outposts were no longer possible. The Briggs Plan had exerted control over the population and broken the big battalions of the enemy. This was arguably the turning point of the war. Having achieved all that had been asked of him Briggs returned to England where, tragically, he died only a few months later.

Even though it is easy to see in retrospect that the end of 1951 was a turning point, neither the Government nor the people realized it at the time. Shaken by the assassination of Gurney and the departure of Briggs, it was decided to combine the posts of High Commissioner and Director of Operations. The man chosen for this daunting post was General Sir Gerald Templer. He had been a Divisional Commander during the Second World War and had subsequently been appointed Director of Intelligence, then Director of Operations at the War Office. In both jobs he had followed the progress of the

Malayan Emergency. On his arrival he made no drastic changes. The Briggs Plan was working well and he stuck to it. His special contribution was his ability as an outstanding leader of men who was able to inspire all those who met him with a determination to defeat the enemy.

An incident on 25th March 1952 just over a month after Templer's arrival in Malaya serves to illustrate his brand of leadership. Fifty miles north of Kuala Lumpur was the town Tanjong Malim. The town's water pipeline had been cut for the sixth time by a platoon of the MRLA. A repair party escorted by some police had been ambushed on its way out to mend the pipeline. Twelve were killed. Templer arrived at Tanjong Malim and spoke to 350 of the townspeople. He ordered the imposition of a twenty-two hours in every twenty-four curfew and instructed each householder to write all that he knew about the local guerilla organization on a slip of paper that would be delivered to his house. These papers, unsigned, were then collected the following day and placed in sealed boxes which were opened by Templer himself in Kuala Lumpur in the presence of witnesses from the offending town. Two weeks later some forty arrests were made as a direct result of the information gained. The curfew was lifted and the guerilla platoon that had committed the atrocity split up and left the area. For the remaining years of the war Tanjong Malim lived in relative peace and security. The story illustrates perfectly Templer's determination to reach the hearts and minds of the people.

In the spring of 1952 the Government forces went on to the offensive. The number of regular units at Templer's disposal remained at twenty-six; however he determined to enlarge the Malayan contribution to the military effort. He raised a sixth battalion of the Malay Regiment and, in order to widen the multi-racial basis of the army, the Federal Regiment was created to enlist Malayan citizens other than Malays. The Home Guard was strengthened substantially and issued with automatic weapons – a demonstration of trust which was to pay enormous dividends. The Government offensive was aimed initially at the MCP branches now forced to live in the jungle due to the success of the Resettlement Programme. Any government success against the MCP branches in turn affected the fighting strength of MRLA units since it was they who had to provide replacements for the losses incurred by the MCP branches. The Communists gave priority to the MCP branches because if any branch ceased to be viable the Chinese villages for which it was responsible would be lost to the cause. Similarly the fighting units could do nothing without the branch. It would get no food, supplies, information or guides. The MCP was the vital link and so became the main target of the security forces.

Once the tide began to turn, the guerilla's hatred for Communism grew. The Party was responsible for the predicament in which he found himself and so the Party's representative in the local MCP branch who had kept him in the jungle became the focal point for his hatred. He knew that unless these men were eliminated he himself would be killed. The Government capitalized on this situation and launched a massive psychological warfare operation which included bribery, amnesties, voice aircraft broadcasting propaganda or dropping leaflets and any other means that paid dividends. The response was staggering and the willingness of Surrendered Enemy Personnel (or SEPs as they became known) to guide patrols to the jungle camps of their former comrades amazed even the phlegmatic British soldier. SEPs were generously rewarded for their information and many subsequently established successful businesses with their blood money and became staunch supporters of the establishment. In May 1953 a force known as the Special Operational Volunteers and consisting of graduates from rehabilitation centres were formed and began to operate effectively against the terrorists.

At the same time many successful operations were mounted by British regiments resulting directly from information supplied by SEPs. One such operation resulted from the surrender of a Min Yuen leader, one Nam Fook, on the morning of 11th June 1952. In return for an offer of money he immediately agreed to lead a patrol of the Green Howards commanded by a Captain Bagnall* to a jungle camp in the Tampin area in the State of Negri Sembilan. Having been led to the camp, Bagnall made a detailed reconnaissance and

---

* Now General Sir Nigel Bagnall KCB, CVO, MC, C.-in-C. British Army of the Rhine.

decided to launch his attack at dawn the following morning. During the night he managed to manoeuvre his platoon to the very perimeter of the enemy camp so that he was able to open fire with devastating effect and total surprise at dawn. Seven terrorists were killed in the hail of bullets and Nam Fook collected a handsome bounty.

After a tour of over three years the Green Howards left Malaya in October 1952. They had accounted for 103 terrorists and their own losses amounted to only one officer and eight men killed in action. It was the infantryman with his rifle on patrol that accounted for the vast majority of enemy kills. Although heavy bombers, artillery and even Royal Naval ships were used to pound the jungle with high explosive these means of mass destruction were largely ineffectual. Later in the war, however, more effective techniques of pinpoint bombing were developed. In February 1956 a patrol was able to fix with great accuracy the precise location of an enemy camp. Five bombers were able to fly straight and low in over the camp and, without any warning, drop seventy 1,000-lb bombs. Fourteen out of the twenty-one guerillas in the camp were killed. In 1957 a technique that allowed bombers to be guided to enemy camp locations at night by radar was developed and proved even more effective as it caught guerillas while they were sleeping. Successful attacks were, however, few and far between since the combination of circumstances necessary for success were difficult to achieve.

Although the Green Howards had been very successful during their three years in Malaya, no other British battalion killed as many terrorists as the 1st Battalion the Suffolk Regiment. When they departed for England in January 1953 after a two-and-a-half-year tour they had accounted for 195 terrorists and suffered a loss themselves of only twelve killed and twenty-four wounded. This regiment was involved in many actions but perhaps their greatest achievement was the slaying of Liew Kon Kim in the Kuala Langat swamp near Kajang in July 1952. Intelligence had indicated the terrorist leader's presence in the swamp which was promptly sealed off by police, home guardsmen and other troops. The Suffolks assisted by two companies of the Royal West Kent Regiment then launched themselves into the swamp. B Company of the

Suffolks commanded by Major Malcolm Dewar* mounted an operation to comb systematically that part of the Kuala Langat swamp in which the latest intelligence indicated Liew Kon Kim was hiding. After six days their perseverance paid off. A patrol led by a National Service officer, 2nd Lieutenant Hands, suddenly came across three terrorists who turned and ran. Hands himself immediately shot the nearest dead and then gave chase to the other two through the swamp. He overtook the second, a woman, who, since she was armed, he also shot dead. By now totally exhausted but determined to finish the job he splashed through the swamp and saw the third figure ahead of him. Again he fired a burst with his Patchet gun and killed the man instantly. When he pulled the bloodied body out of the muddy water he immediately recognized the bearded face of the man whom the Suffolks had been chasing for two years – the notorious leader of the Kajang gang, the 'bearded wonder' himself, Liew Kon Kim. Hands was awarded the MC for this action and Dewar the OBE.

The pressure on the rebels continued throughout 1953. Sikorsky helicopters of 848 Naval Air Squadron introduced a new element of flexibility into operations in March, though their use was both limited and of an experimental nature. They were used in operations to support the 1st and 3rd King's African Rifles (KAR), the 2/6th and 2/10th Gurkhas and the Manchesters and achieved varying degrees of success. This early use of helicopters had a limited impact on operations due to the limited pay load of the Sikorsky, the need for the soldiers carried in them to descend down a rope into the jungle, and also because there were only a total of ten troop-carrying helicopters available in Malaya. Perhaps the most effective use of these helicopters was to deposit small groups of 22 SAS deep in the jungle to win over the hearts and minds of the Aborigine tribes and to protect them from intimidation by the terrorists. In April the 1st KAR returned to Kenya; in July the Worcestershire Regiment was replaced by the West Yorkshires and in September the 2/2nd Gurkhas returned to Hong Kong. These moves produced a significant

*Malcolm Dewar, now Lt-Colonel Malcolm Dewar OBE (Retd), is the author's father.

change: for the first time Malaya became the largest
contributor of infantry battalions to the war effort. By October
there were eight Malayan battalions, seven British, seven
Gurkha, one African and one Fijian. Templer had achieved
what he had set out to do and so on 30th May 1954 he left
Kuala Lumpur for London taking with him the gratitude and
affection of the vast bulk of the Malayan people.

The process of pacification was well under way by the time
Templer left. Parts of Malacca, Trengganu, Kedah and Negri
Sembilan had been declared 'white' between September 1953
and March 1954. This indicated that they were free of terrorist
intimidation and firmly under Government control. However
before he left Templer emphasized that there were over 4,000
terrorists left in the jungle. There was still much work to do.

When Templer departed, the offices of High Commissioner
and Director of Operations were again separated. The former
post was inherited by Sir Donald MacGillivray and the latter by
Lt-General Sir Geoffrey Bourne. Bourne adopted the strategy
of concentrating on those areas where the Communist
organization was weakest, mostly in the eastern and central
parts of Malaya where the Chinese population was smallest.
His aim was to declare these areas 'white' as soon as
practicable so that he could then concentrate his available
forces on the blacker areas. It was the classic stratagem of
defeating the enemy in detail. Once an area was declared
'white' curfews, food rationing and all the other paraphernalia
of the Emergency Regulations were lifted. The area was
supervised only by the police and the Home Guard and the
troops were moved on to remaining problem areas. Once an
area was declared 'white' the local population ensured that it
remained so.

The worst areas were the rubber and tin states along the
western side of the peninsula and most of these were not
cleared until 1958–9. Massive concentrations of troops
sometimes produced a miserable return. One such operation
was mounted in the Ipoh area between July and November
1954. It involved RAF bombers, 22 SAS, and four infantry
battalions. Only fifteen rebels were killed.

The most important aspect of a Federal priority operation
was not so much killing terrorists (if they could be found) but

finding food dumps and to collect evidence to use against the Min Yuen. After months of collecting and collating evidence a massive police swoop aimed to arrest all suppliers of food in the area of the operation. The rationing of food was intensified so that it was virtually impossible to put some aside for the guerillas. Food was sold either pre-cooked (so that it would only last 24 hours) or in opened tins. MCP branches were then forced to recruit replacements for the Min Yuen thereby taking 'risks that they would not otherwise have taken. During the first few months of these operations, there were few kills. The immediate reward for the security forces was hunger for the guerillas and evidence for the Special Branch – the kills came though, in the fullness of time.

In August 1955 the 1/10 Gurkhas became the first and only battalion to kill 300 rebels. Typical of the high standard of marksmanship and physical fitness demonstrated by this battalion over the years was the amazing feat of Rifleman Birbahadur Rai who was awarded the DCM for his efforts. His platoon was involved in a contact with a group of terrorists in an oil-palm plantation on the jungle fringe. The terrorists appeared to be setting up a temporary camp for the night. Visibility between the palms was good and it was possible to see in places for up to a hundred yards. The terrorists, clearly outnumbered, scattered and ran. Birbahadur, armed with a Patchet carbine, gave chase and after two hundred yards caught up with the nearest terrorist who was firing an automatic weapon in his direction. Birbahadur shot the man dead and then ran on into the camp where he shot two more terrorists dead as they attempted to escape. Running on down what appeared to be the terrorists' escape route back into the jungle he suddenly came face to face with another Chinese terrorist who he also killed while under fire himself. By now exhausted, he glimpsed another running figure about seventy-five yards away whom he felled with a last well aimed shot. Such was the marksmanship and determination which made the Gurkha soldier so feared by the Communists.

In December 1955 a meeting near the Thai border was arranged between Chin Peng and Tunku Abdul Rahman, the newly elected Chief Minister of the Federation. Despite the generous amnesty terms offered by the Government the negotiations broke down. Soon after the Tunku was informed by the British Government that Malaya would be granted independence by August 1957. The feet were knocked from under the terrorists. No longer could they pretend they were fighting to liberate Malaya.

In May 1956 Bourne handed over to a new Director of Operations, Lt-General Bower. He inherited command of twenty-four infantry battalions, of which eight were British. Wales was represented by the 2nd Royal Welch Fusiliers and the 1st South Wales Borderers and Scotland by the Royal Scots Fusiliers and the 1st King's Own Scottish Borderers. One of the English battalions, the Royal Hampshire Regiment, handed over to the Rifle Brigade in August 1956. The Hampshires will be remembered for one of the most successful operations of the Malayan Emergency. In December 1955, acting on information obtained by the Special Branch from a deserter, a company of the Hampshires mounted an operation to attack a terrorist camp in Selangor where some terrorist leaders were attending a course of political indoctrination. The assault was highly successful, eleven out of the twelve terrorists in the camp were killed and the only survivor, the secretary of the Ulu Langat branch of the Communist Party, was captured a few days later.

Independence Day came on 31st August 1957. The Tunku announced a general amnesty for all terrorists during his inaugural speech. Six weeks after Independence Day five terrorists, one of whom was the regional political commissar for the whole of South Perak, surrendered to the local police station. An agreement was worked out whereby for every ten guerillas he brought in he would be rewarded with the sum of 20,000 Malayan dollars. For six months, the surrender was kept secret as the commissar branch by branch, district by district, led in the entire Communist hierarchy of the South Perak region. He was able to do this over such a long period of time because the Communist cell system means that each branch is oblivious of what the others are doing except when informed through official channels by the commissar himself, and that might be only every two or three months. The Special Branch cleverly exploited what is normally regarded as the main strength of the Communist system. A second 'super grass' accounted for most of the Communist command structure in the Johore area in April 1958. Despite these successes the war continued unabated after Independence Day. The continued efforts of the Security Forces and the increasing rate of terrorist surrenders meant that by August the north and centre of Johore were declared 'white'. Now overwhelming resources could be concentrated in the remaining black areas of North Perak and South Johore. By December 1959 the Loyals were the only British battalion still operational. When they departed that month they had accounted for seventeen Communist terrorists which, during the latter stages, was no mean achievement. Among their victims was Sin Mah, the leader of the gang that had murdered Sir Henry Gurney. On 31st July 1960 the State of Emergency was officially declared to be ended. Chin Peng, with a small band of loyal supporters, survived the war and is said to live to this day in the jungle just north of the Malay-Thai border.

It took twelve years to defeat Communist insurgency. The campaign was in many ways an object lesson in successful anti-guerilla operations which sadly has not been repeated very often since. Though the backing of regular troops, aircraft and relatively sophisticated equipment was a vital ingredient in defeating insurgency, success could not have been achieved without the wholehearted participation of the indigenous population – the Federal Army, the Home Guard, the Police Force, the Malayan Chinese Special Branch double agents and the bulk of the civilian population itself. By the end of the war the police force numbered 67,000 and the Home Guard 350,000. Some 3,000 civilians, 1,350 policemen and 128 Malayan soldiers lost their lives during the war. British Army casualties were seventy officers, 280 men and 159 Gurkhas killed. Of the 12,000 members of the MRLA who had opposed the security forces throughout the Emergency, 6,710 were killed, 2,696 surrendered, 2,820 were wounded and 1,290 captured. The remaining thousand died of disease or malnutrition, or deserted or were executed by their own commanders.

Communism was beaten not only by military measures and the Emergency Regulations but also by winning the hearts and minds of the people. Of all those who influenced the course of the war, Briggs, Templer, and Tunku Abdul Rahman deserve pride of place – Briggs for the Briggs Plan which laid the foundations for victory, Templer for his imaginative leadership of the people and skilled management of the security forces, and the Tunku for his patience, perseverance and perception in leading the Malayan people to independence against all odds. The guerillas were defeated in the jungle because the British Army was willing to beat the guerillas at their own game. They were willing to live and fight in the jungle for long periods of time relying for the most part on no other weapons than rifles and light machine guns. Massive and indiscriminate firepower is seldom the answer in the jungle. Rather the prerequisites for success are low cunning among commanders and superb standards of minor infantry tactics among soldiers. A hundred thousand British soldiers served in Malaya during the twelve years of the Emergency and the vast majority were National Servicemen. Their success in Malaya was one of the finest achievements of the British Army since 1945.

4

British Honduras/Belize
1948-83

In 1945 the only British military presence in the Caribbean was
one infantry battalion stationed in Kingston, Jamaica. One
company was normally detached to the island of Bermuda.
Part of the widespread responsibilities of Headquarters
Caribbean Area was the small British colony of British
Honduras situated on the east coast of Central America.
British Honduras has been a colony since the Anglo-Spanish
treaty of 1786; initially its vast resources of mahogany proved a
vital asset to the Royal Navy. It became however a sleepy and
forgotten corner of the Empire. The country possesses few
other natural resources; sugar, rice and tropical fruits were
exported and there have been attempts to find oil, as yet
unsuccessful. But the economy remained for the most part
based on subsistence agriculture.

Both Guatemala and Mexico have laid claim to British
Honduras since the early nineteenth century. Mexico has never
pressed her claim to the north of the colony. In 1945 however
Guatemala published a new constitution which referred to
British Honduras as an integral part of the State of Guatemala.
In late February 1948 the Guatemalans threatened to invade.
The British Government ordered HQ Caribbean Area to
dispatch troops of the 2nd Battalion the Gloucestershire
Regiment to the colony immediately. Two companies from the
battalion landed in Belize City from the cruiser HMS *Devonshire*
on 2nd March. One of these companies deployed to the border
where it found no sign of a Guatemalan incursion. The threat
was taken seriously however and it was decided to station one
company in Belize City permanently.

3 Central America. The strategic position of British Honduras (now Belize) is evident

Belize City is sadly no substitute for Bermuda. It was built in 1920 after a hurricane had destroyed the previous capital in 1911. Except for three stone-built churches, the capital is a shanty town. Its population of 50,000 forms nearly a third of the total population of 140,000. The coastal areas are inhabited by Creoles, Spanish, Caribs, Lebanese and a few Europeans of North American extraction and the forests further inland mostly by Mayan Indians. In addition there are two small colonies of Mennonites, some 2–3,000 men, women and children in all, originally from Holland and Germany but more recently religious refugees from North America, who run highly successful communal farms providing much of the food and dairy produce for Belize City.

The coastline is mangrove, the interior forest and the climate sub-tropical. The hurricane season persists from July to November during which it is possible to experience thirty-six inches of rain in ten days. Such was the environment that the Gloucesters swopped for the sun-drenched beaches of Bermuda a thousand miles to their north-east.

After the scare of 1948 British Honduras resumed its role as the least well known corner of the Empire. There was another scare in 1957 when Guatemala made threatening noises and an additional company of the Worcestershire Regiment was dispatched on board HMS *Ulster* from Kingston. On their arrival the Guatemalans as usual denied that there was a problem. After a brief stay carrying out jungle training the additional Worcester company returned to Kingston. Then on 31st October 1961 Hurricane 'Hattie' hit Belize City. Some 400 people were killed and 65,000 made homeless. A company of the 1st Battalion the Hampshire Regiment stationed at Airport Camp just outside Belize City worked ceaselessly for days on end to restore the situation until on 3rd November or soon after the rest of the battalion supported by Royal Navy and US Navy detachments arrived to provide much needed reinforcements. The 1st Battalion the Worcestershire Regiment and 12 Field Squadron of the Royal Engineers were rushed out from England in mid-November to provide additional relief before returning home for Christmas, their task completed. Though Belize City was rebuilt the capital was moved to Belmopan further inland.

On 21st January the following year news reached the Hampshires, now reduced to one resident company again, that a small force had crossed the border from Guatemala and raised the Guatemalan flag on British territory. The platoon that was sent to the area located the intruders and some shots were exchanged. It transpired however that 'the invaders' were not Guatemalan soldiers but 'Belize Freedom Fighters' who no doubt had received aid and encouragement from across the border but who were badly organized and ineffective. Some twenty members of the 'Belize Liberation Army' were rounded up and sent for trial. Again British Honduras drifted back into obscurity.

When Jamaica became independent in 1962 HQ Caribbean Area ceased to exist. The company in British Honduras was now provided by a battalion in England. This was initially the Duke of Wellington's Regiment, who were followed during the sixties by the King's Shropshire Light Infantry and the Staffordshire Regiment. In 1970 the Guatemalans became increasingly bellicose again about their claim to the colony. As a precaution the Spearhead Battalion, the Gloucesters, plus some men of the Devon and Dorset Regiment were flown to Belize, as the colony had by now become known, so that within days there was a reinforced battalion *in situ* to demonstrate to the Guatemalans that the British Government meant business. Once again the situation was defused though for some years the troop level remained at an infantry battalion reinforced with an additional company.

Then in 1977 the Guatemalans actually moved troops to the border. The decision was now taken to put on a considerable show of strength. A second battalion was immediately dispatched to Belize. This was supported by a Close Reconnaissance troop consisting of Scimitar and Scorpion armoured vehicles armed respectively with 30-mm Rarden cannons and 76-mm guns, one Field Battery equipped with 105-mm Light Guns, several Blowpipe low level surface-to-air missile detachments and a squadron of engineers. In addition the RAF flew six Harrier vertical take-off fighters into Belize airfield. These were protected by Rapier missiles. A Royal Naval frigate on the Caribbean station sailed close in to the coastline near Stann Creek to provide cover against air attack for the Battalion Group stationed in the South. When the Harriers landed warlike noises emanating from Guatemala City ceased instantly.

Since 1977 the border has been patrolled regularly and permanent observation posts set up at key points overlooking Guatemala. Relations with the Guatemalan Army have, by and large, been extremely friendly. Regular meetings have taken place in the border area between the Guatemalan sappers

1 Aftermath of the
bombing of the
King David Hotel in
Jerusalem

2 British soldiers
with illegal
immigrants in Haifa
1947

3 A lesson in tactics in the Malayan jungle

4 Troops prepare a 'helipad' during the campaign in Malaya

5 Irish Rangers guard a Harrier vertical take-off aircraft near Belize city

6 A Puma helicopter lifts troops of the 2nd Battalion the Royal Irish Rangers from their base camp near Belize city to the area of the border with Guatemala

7 Major-General H.E.M. Bredin meets a Guatemalan soldier on the border at the site of the East-West road, which was the cause of friction February/March 1980
8 Strangled victim of the Mau Mau in the Abedare Forest in the Kenyan Highlands

9 National
Servicemen round
up Mau Mau
terrorist suspects

10 Troops
prepare a meal in
the forest in
British Guiana

11 Greenjackets instruct
Guiana Defence Force
soldiers in the use of an
A41 radio

12 EOKA terrorists in the
Cyprus mountains showing
Grivas (front left) and
Ioannu (behind him) who
was captured with this
photograph by the 2nd
Battalion the Parachute
Regiment, 15th June 1957

ΓΑΛΑ ΒΛΑΧ

13 Members of the Royal Berkshire Regiment on a 'cat patrol' in Nicosia in search of EOKA terrorists, November 1958

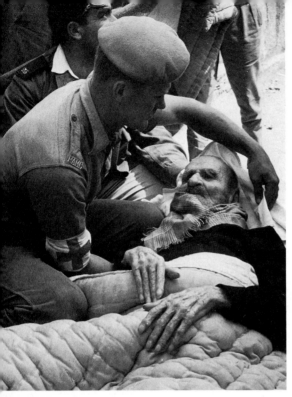

14 The Royal Army Medical Corps give aid to an injured Greek Cypriot, April 1964

15 Cameronians, Oman Scouts and the Sultan's troops gather around a well at Izz, the first rebel village to capitulate during the advance on Nizwa, August 1957

building a road to the Belize border and British troops ensuring the border is not violated. The basis for all negotiations has been the treaty between Guatemala and Great Britain which was signed on 30th April 1859 confirming the existing line of the border. The boundary between the two countries was partially marked by a Captain Wray in 1881 though not finished by an Assistant Surveyor Miller until 1887. The line marked by Miller was agreed in an exchange of notes between the two governments in 1931 and 1933. Survey work completed by the army in the last few years has brought to light several possibly unintentional incursions by the Guatemalan engineers; in one instance a main road recently constructed by the Guatemalans stops fifty metres inside Belize and the pilot road some 300 metres. Tactful negotiation by officers of the 2nd King Edward VII's Own Gurkha Rifles, the Black Watch, the Cheshire Regiment and the Irish Rangers in the past six years has resolved most of these problems. By March 1980 C Company of the 2nd Battalion the Royal Irish Rangers had struck up a working relationship with their opposite numbers in the 1st Battalion the Poptun Brigade. It is largely the efforts of British officers to defuse the situation by negotiation that has allowed the Ministry of Defence to reduce the garrison to a four-company battalion.

Apart from a brief scare in April 1982, when it was thought that the Guatemalans might take advantage of the Falklands War to invade, Belize has remained quiet.

The country was granted its independence in 1981. The British Government has agreed that the British Army will remain in Belize for 'an appropriate period' to safeguard the territorial integrity of the newly emergent nation. The intention is to strengthen the Belize Defence Force so that at some time in the future Belize will be able to provide for its own defence. Whatever the outcome, there is little doubt that the British Army has made a valuable contribution towards the future stability of an independent Belize. The role of the army in Belize has never been a glamorous one and only a very few shots have been fired in anger; this in itself is a great tribute to the ingenuity and discipline of the many regiments who have served in this forgotten corner of Empire. The main lesson of Belize has been that a few troops in time save a great deal more trouble later. If for no other reason Belize is important because it has demonstrated that deterrence can and does work.

5

Kenya
1952-56

The Mau Mau Rebellion in Kenya, which erupted so violently in late 1952, can only really be understood by tracing the changes in control, use and condition of the land in that country since 1885 when a conference in Berlin, at which interested European states were represented, marked out interior Africa for colonization.

In East Africa the British started their colonization of what is now Kenya from Mombasa. The intention was to gain control of Lake Victoria. *En route* they had to cross the Kenya Highlands and, as an aid to holding the route to Lake Victoria, settlement of the highlands was encouraged. Quite apart from more positive motives, it was important to forestall French moves up the Nile towards the great African Lakes and to rival the German push inland to Lake Victoria through the territory which subsequently became the British mandated territory of Tanganyika after the Great War. British settlers therefore established cattle and grain farms and plantations of coffee, tea, sisal, wattle and other tropical crops. Much of this happened before 1915. Some of the land was purchased from African owners and some obtained by grant from the British Government from lands that had been declared Crown property.

When the British colonized the highlands between Mombasa and Lake Victoria several tribes lived there. The nomadic Masai, who had first appeared in the area in the early nineteenth century, occupied small spots of land within the vast territory over which they roamed and from which they

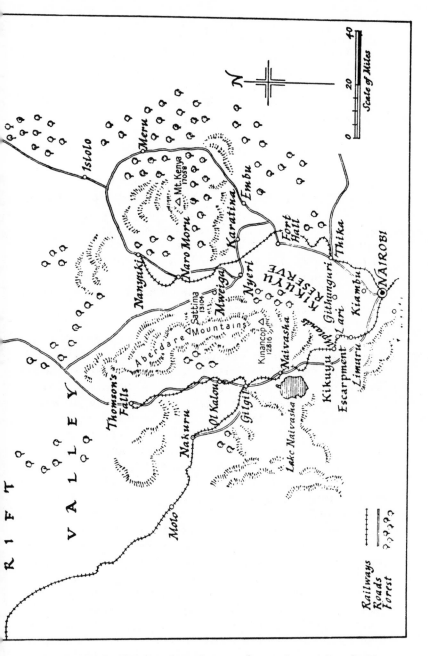

4 The Highlands of Kenya; the main area of operations against the Mau Mau in Kenya 1952-56

excluded other tribes. Since the Masai never tilled their soil and held much more land than they needed, they made treaties with the British Government surrendering thousands of square miles of land suitable for European farming. The ceded lands form a large part of the 17,000 square miles which have since become known as 'The White Highlands'. A small part of the highlands had in fact never been used by any Africans. The remainder was obtained mainly from the Kikuyu, a tribe that had lived by the system known as shifting cultivation. The Kikuyu owners had originally bought the land from weak local tribes. When Europeans in turn purchased the land from Kikuyu owners they assumed they were buying the land freehold but because they did not conduct the purchase in the manner required by Kikuyu custom, the Kikuyu assumed the Europeans were only renting the land for a limited period.

The European community developed an extremely high standard of living over the years and nowhere was the contrast between African and European standards more obvious than in the area in and around Nairobi which was situated on the edge of the highlands. The Kikuyu tribal territory was in fact the only Reserve that was intermeshed with the prosperous and sparsely populated White Highlands. No other Kenya tribe has been in such close proximity for so long with Europeans. As some Kikuyu became more politically aware after the Second World War, the land issue became a serious grievance. The European farmers not surprisingly refused to relinquish lands which they had developed and which the claimants had never owned. Out of this land dispute grew the Mau Mau Rebellion.

In September and October 1952 a number of Africans loyal to the Government were murdered; numerous reports of oathing and intimidation were received and on European farms cattle were maimed and buildings burned down. The new Governor, Sir Evelyn Baring, arrived in Kenya on 29th September and within three weeks he had decided that he had no alternative but to declare a State of Emergency. In calling for British military aid he declared war on the terrorists. Although it is difficult to see what else he could have done, this move created a large number of recruits to the insurgent cause. Mau Mau oaths became more extreme in their commitment and in the degree of violence they generated.

The call for British military aid was answered on 19th

October when the first elements of the 1st Battalion the Lancashire Fusiliers arrived from Egypt in Valetta aircraft. That night the police rounded up eighty-three suspected Mau Mau leaders, Jomo Kenyatta among them. At first there was little reaction. It looked as if the Mau Mau had responded to this show of force in the manner which the Governor had hoped. However after only a few weeks the Mau Mau took the offensive probably mostly as a result of the forced return of large numbers of Kikuyu squatters and labour from the Rift Valley farms to the overcrowded Kikuyu reserves. Throughout November and December and the first few months of 1953 they carried out a series of attacks, many of them successful, on European farmers and Africans loyal to the Government. Then on 26th March a large band of insurgents killed at least seventy-four people (a further fifty were missing believed killed), mostly women and children, at the village of Lari only twenty-five miles from Nairobi. As if the Lari massacre, as it subsequently became known, was not enough, on the same night the insurgents attacked a fortified police post at Naivasha killing two policemen, releasing 150 prisoners and stealing a large number of weapons. This deterioration in the security situation led directly to the request for further military aid and the arrival of more British battalions. In May General Sir George Erskine was appointed Commander-in-Chief of all military units. He was also given operational control of the police and auxiliary troops. His command consisted of 39 Brigade (either two or three battalions of British troops), 70 Brigade (either five or six battalions of King's African Rifles) as well as the all-European Kenya Regiment, the East African Independent Armoured Car Squadron, a battery of the East African Artillery and two RAF Squadrons, one of Harvards and one of Lincolns.

When the Lancashire Fusiliers arrived in September 1952 they were the first British troops to serve in sub-Saharan Africa in time of peace for forty years. Neither they nor their commanders really knew what to expect. They were not properly trained or equipped for operations in Kenya – and it showed. Most battalions arrived straight from Britain but even those deployed from Malaya found the forests of Kenya very different from the Malayan jungle; and jungle green uniform was most unsuitable for the cold nights in the highlands. As in

Malaya battalions were composed of conscripts; young officers were woefully inexperienced and for the most part untrained in the techniques of forest warfare. Things improved as the campaign progressed but there is little doubt that some dreadful mistakes were made. Men of the King's Shropshire Light Infantry ambushed and killed their own Commanding Officer, though it should be said that he walked through an ambush that had been set – a fatal error on his part.

A committee system based on the Malayan model was evolved at District and later at higher levels to co-ordinate military, police and civil affairs. The system tended to create friction between the military and the European settlers. The latter required protection and the military were naturally keen not to get bogged down in static duties but to take the offensive in the forests. Nevertheless on the whole it worked well.

After the arrival of 39 Brigade the country was divided into classified areas. The Aberdares and Mount Kenya, uninhabited forest and mountain, were classified as Prohibited Areas. The Prohibited Areas included a strip one mile wide along the eastern edge of the Aberdares and a similar strip on the south and east sides of Mount Kenya. These strips were controlled by police and army patrols and camps. Within the prohibited areas the Security Forces were able to operate on a war footing; troops were able to open fire on sight.

Most of the remaining areas of Kenya were designated Special Areas. Within these troops had the right to halt and question, to open fire if a challenge was ignored and to open fire on sight during the hours of curfew. Although the Government was accorded the widest powers these powers did not replace the basis of Common Law with Martial Law.

Erskine tended at first to be overconfident. Although the terrain was daunting, the enemy appeared to be badly led and indifferently trained. There were only 12,000 guerillas in early 1953 and they had no support outside Kenya. Very few were armed with proper firearms and none had had any military or revolutionary training abroad. However the terrain was more of a problem than he at first imagined and was perhaps the main factor in prolonging the war. The Aberdares are over sixty miles long. They rise to 13,000 feet in places. Up to about 9,000 feet the slopes are covered in dense forest; at about 11,000 feet the bamboo gives way to moorland covered in jungle grass and is interspersed with streams and rivers. With the advantage of hindsight it is perhaps not surprising that working in an almost impenetrable forest at a considerable altitude presented serious problems to the British troops. Moreover the insurgents' logistic support was excellent. Their lines of supply for food, money, recruits, information and medical supplies stretched across the Kikuyu tribal lands and even into Nairobi. British soldiers on the other hand had to overcome their own clumsiness while pitted against an enemy who, whatever his limitations, possessed an acute sense of smell, hearing and stealth. After a short time in Kenya, Erskine realized that perhaps it would not be over in a matter of months.

During May 1953 the Devons were involved in several clashes in the Aberdares. By the end of the month they had killed eight terrorists, captured two, and recovered some of the rifles taken by the terrorists in the raid on Naivasha Police Station in March. Then in June a co-ordinated operation in the Aberdares involving several battalions and the support of Harvard bombers resulted in the death or capture of over fifty Mau Mau. The documents captured during the operation showed that the 15,000 or so Mau Mau fighters were organized in platoons and battalions under the leadership of terrorists with absurdly pretentious titles. One of the Mau Mau leaders described himself as Prime Minister of the Kenya Parliament, Commander in Chief of the Kikuyu and Mumbi Trinity Armies and Townswatch Battalions, President of the Kenya Young Stars Association, President of the Kikuyu and Mumbi Itungati Association, President of the Kenya African Women's League and Chairman of the Kinyarikalo Memorial Club! Even more worrying were the nearly one million sworn supporters. Operations continued throughout July with varying degrees of success. Then in August the Lancashire Fusiliers, who had been the first British battalion to deploy in Kenya after the Governor's appeal for military aid, returned home to England. They were replaced by the Black Watch who after only a few days, found themselves operating in the Aberdares next to the Devons.

Erskine soon realized that he would need still more battalions. In late September, 49 Brigade consisting of only two battalions, namely the Northumberland Fusiliers and the

Royal Inniskilling Fusiliers, were deployed to the lower slopes of Mount Kenya where the Meru and Embu tribes were succumbing to Mau Mau intimidation. Meanwhile the King's African Rifle (KAR) battalions were in general kept in Kikuyuland or the white settled areas; however they also supported British troops in the Mount Kenya area.

The concentration of security forces soon began to pay dividends. A joint force of British troops and Kikuyu Guard eliminated a strong insurgent group in November; early in 1954 several insurgent groups were destroyed by the police in the Karatina area and then in February British and KAR troops supported by police and Kikuyu Guard killed 126 insurgents and captured eighteen in a running battle lasting four days between Thika and Murang'a. The successes were spoiled by the death on Christmas Eve 1953 of Major the Earl Wavell, only son of Field Marshal Wavell of Second World War fame, who was shot dead during anti-Mau Mau operations near Thika.

As a result of the success of these operations the first Mau Mau started to take advantage of the surrender offer made by the Government which provided an amnesty for those who had carried arms or consorted with the insurgents. After a slow start the scheme produced over 800 surrenders by 17th January 1955.

On 24th April 1954 Erskine initiated Operation Anvil involving five British battalions. Its aim was to purge Nairobi of Mau Mau. The entire city was cordoned before dawn and the population taken completely by surprise. For twelve days roads were blocked and houses searched; over 16,500 men and women were removed to the screening camp at Langata and thence to one of the huge detention camps in the Coast Province. The operation succeeded in shattering the city's Mau Mau hierarchy and cells, and inevitably affected the lines of communication with the insurgents in the forest. Outside Nairobi 'villagization', on the Malayan model, was enforced in particularly hostile areas; in other areas attempts were made with varying degrees of success to persuade the inhabitants to accept villagization in return for a promise of improved social services. Throughout the remainder of the year large-scale screening operations involving both British battalions and KAR were carried out in the Thika, Murang'a and Kiambu areas. Various small-scale actions also took place in the Meru Embu and Nyeri districts including one involving the Devons in August in which a Mau Mau gang stood its ground and fought ferociously – a fairly unusual phenomenon. Major Hastings led a charge against the insurgents and was promptly knocked to the ground by a bullet. He continued to engage the enemy from the ground with his Patchet gun at the same time issuing orders. The action resulted in the killing of two high-ranking Mau Mau. When the enemy eventually scattered Major Hastings had to be carried through eight miles of forest to reach the nearest airstrip. He was awarded the DSO for his bravery and leadership during the action.

At the end of the year both the Buffs and the Devons, who had borne the brunt of the Kenya Campaign, were relieved by the 1st King's Own Yorkshire Light Infantry and the 1st Rifle Brigade. Both departing battalions had had considerable success against the insurgents though the Devons encountered stiffer opposition. The Buffs were able to claim 290 Mau Mau killed and 194 captured for the loss of only one man killed. The Devons, on the other hand, lost five killed and six wounded and achieved fewer kills. The New Year saw a greater emphasis on offensive operations in the forest areas. Continual sweeps, patrolling and ambushing, although they did not result in great numbers of enemy casualties, kept the Mau Mau on the move. Their lines of supply and communication were disrupted and they were forced more and more to raid indiscriminately to obtain supplies. This inevitably led to a loss in popularity among the Kikuyu. At the same time the Kikuyu Guard became increasingly dependable to the extent that it was possible to issue them with firearms. The trust put in the Kikuyu by the Government paid enormous dividends. The Guard formed an effective counter-balance within the Kikuyu tribe to the Mau Mau. They worked with British and KAR battalions as guides and large areas of tribal lands were eventually entrusted to their protection. There is little doubt that they played a decisive role in defeating insurgency in Kenya. However there was abuse of power among the Guard. Consequently Erskine was forced to reduce the force from its ceiling of 25,000 and re-enrol some of its members as tribal policemen and tribal police reserve, a move which was completed by mid-1955.

In January 1955 the 1st Royal Irish Fusiliers arrived closely followed by the 1st Gloucestershire Regiment. There were now six British and six KAR battalions available for operations.

It was at this stage that General Erskine handed over command to a new Commander-in-Chief. His successor was Lt-General G.W. Lathbury. By using the somewhat plodding but effective and certainly appropriate tactic of attrition, Erskine had succeeded in forcing the Mau Mau to operate in smaller and more disjointed groups. For what the statistics are worth over 8,000 Mau Mau had been killed, nearly 1,000 captured and 22,500 placed in detention. However many of the gang leaders were still at large – it was just that their gangs were smaller and that they had lost the initiative. In spite of their increasingly heavy losses, the aims of the militant Mau Mau and their sympathizers in the Kikuyu, Embu and Meru tribes had not really altered. Now that they realized that the European population could not be ejected by force, their policy was to survive as long as was necessary to force an exhausted and economically crippled Kenya Government to grant concessions. To this end their tactics were now to avoid contact with the security forces but to cause sufficient trouble to ensure their continued deployment. The number of terrorists still active in the forests was now estimated to be approximately 5,000 with about 800 precision weapons among them.

Lathbury soon realized that conventional military measures on their own were unlikely to flush out the smaller and more elusive gangs. He therefore decided that the time was ripe to put greater emphasis on the special forces tactics initiated under Erskine some eighteen months previously. The system of using turned ex-gangsters as pseudo-gangsters was developed by a young Field Intelligence Officer, a Major Frank Kitson of the Rifle Brigade.* Kitson had stumbled on the idea while interrogating a captured terrorist who showed a remarkable willingness to turn informer on his erstwhile comrades – a practice which had also been exploited, though in not quite the same way, in Malaya.

---

*Now General Sir Frank Kitson author of *Gangs and Counter Gangs* and of the Foreword to this book.

Lathbury gave his complete support to the pseudo-gang idea which Major Kitson had developed as it soon became increasingly clear that clumsy and costly sweeps involving vast numbers of troops were no longer producing results commensurate with the effort put into them. Some 300–400 mainly former insurgents served in the pseudo-gangs and there were no defections back to the Mau Mau.

Frank Kitson had arrived in Kenya in August 1953. In March the following year he heard that a British Intelligence Officer called Hales who was stationed at Fort Hall had had an extraordinary experience. He had been out in the bush with several of his African helpers when the group suddenly found themselves surrounded by several hundred Mau Mau insurgents. Hales, realizing that he was bound to be recognized, walked a short distance away and crouched down behind some scrub. The Africans with Hales pretended to be Mau Mau supporters and they all – to their amazement – got away with it. Kitson was quick to recognize the significance of this event. Because they did not expect to see a white man they did not notice Hales nor did they seem to doubt that Hales' Africans were Mau Mau supporters. Kitson decided to cash in on the insurgents' gullibility by training Africans, particularly ex-Mau Mau, to impersonate gangsters as a regular means of getting information. He resisted the temptation to use the information for offensive purposes immediately after obtaining it other than in quite exceptional circumstances for fear of prejudicing his whole operation.

Any good leader feels the need to join his men in the field. The fact that his face was white did not deter Kitson from joining his pseudo-gangs on operations whenever he was sure his presence would not endanger the operation or the lives of his men. Occasionally offensive operations were undertaken in which Kitson sometimes took part. His disguise was not elaborate and consisted of wearing an old mackintosh, a blanket around the shoulders, an old African bush hat and a blacked face and hands. On one of these patrols, which consisted of four British Intelligence Officers including Kitson and four Africans including one ex-terrorist guide, the aim was to capture a local gang, the Rift Valley Gang, which was known to be staying the night in some huts about ten miles outside

Nairobi. After dismounting from their landrovers, the patrol walked the last few miles to the terrorist hideout. Kitson, who was at the end of the line, watched fascinated as the Africans in his patrol made contact with the two Mau Mau sentries, who were clearly not suspicious. Kitson and his patrol seized the moment and rushed into the hut shouting and shining their torches in the faces of the occupants who were forced against the far wall and covered with automatic weapons. Within twenty minutes each of the gang had been tied up with ropes. It was soon apparent that the prisoners consisted of the gang leader of the Rift Valley Gang with six of his men as well as the leader and second-in-command of another gang. It was a classic example of the effectiveness of the pseudo-gangs.

By the late summer of 1955 the pseudo-gangs had achieved much of what they had set out to do. The remaining terrorists were so depleted and scattered that it was becoming increasingly difficult for pseudo-gangs to operate successfully. Kitson's last operation in August 1955 ended in the killing of the terrorist leader Waruingi Kurier. After Kitson's departure the pseudo-gangs were directed by Superintendent Ian Henderson until they captured Dedan Kimathi in October 1956, the self-styled Field-Marshal Commanding-in-Chief the Kenya Land and Freedom Armies, Knight Commander of the African Empire and Popular Prime Minister of the Southern Hemisphere. His capture and subsequent execution marked the end of the military campaign in Kenya. The pseudo-gang idea will always stand as one of the more imaginative examples of British military inventiveness. Major Neville Cooper MC Commanding 'I' Company of the Kenya Regiment had also posed as a Mau Mau terrorist and led other white officers as well as locally recruited Africans on pseudo-gang operations from 1953 onwards. While their achievement should in no way be underestimated, it was Frank Kitson who really seized upon the idea and developed it with such success.

As well as giving every support to pseudo-gang operations, Lathbury decided to mount a series of operations against the terrorists in the forests. Operations Gimlet, Dante and Beatrice took place during July and August 1955 in the Aberdares and Mount Kenya areas. 49 Brigade were supported during Operation Dante by Harvard and Lincoln bombers and 3.7-inch shells from the guns of 156 Anti-Aircraft Battery.

Neither the heavy bombers or guns killed many terrorists but they did succeed in unsettling them and keeping them on the move. By 10th August when these operations ended over one hundred terrorists had been accounted for and intelligence reports indicated that the gangs had been further scattered and disorganized. Operation Beatrice was the last large-scale operation mounted during the Kenya Emergency. Lathbury now made the firm decision to withdraw his battalions back to the forest edge. A great ditch was dug around parts of the forest to prevent egress. Both British and KAR battalions limited their operations to local sweeps in settled areas and Kikuyuland. Great emphasis was put on winning the hearts and minds of the local population by staging weapon displays, sport competitions and band displays. Meanwhile tactics employing small-scale operations supported by good intelligence was the rule throughout 1955. These methods succeeded in reducing the numbers of active insurgents to a few hundred hunted and desperate fugitives. Between August and November 1955 39 Brigade was gradually disbanded, this process being completed when the Rifle Brigade was moved from the Aberdares to the Rift Valley area. In December an operation involving the Rifle Brigade, the Gloucesters, the King's Shropshire Light Infantry, the East African Recce Squadron, the Kenya Police and the Kikuyu Guard was launched to clear Lake Naivasha and its surrounding area of the seventy Mau Mau who were supposedly still sheltering there. The operation netted twenty-four killed, captured or surrendered.

In April 1956 the Rifle Brigade departed to serve in Malaya and the Gloucesters to Aden, both to face very different enemies. In May, control of operations was handed over to the police. Directed by Ian Henderson the pseudo-gangs really got into their stride, their efforts culminating in the capture of Kimathi in October. On 2nd November the last British battalion to take part in the Mau Mau Campaign, the King's Shropshire Light Infantry, departed for the Persian Gulf though British troops in fact remained in Kenya until 1965. They were only used once more in anger to suppress the short-lived 1964 Kenya Army Mutiny.

The Emergency was not declared at an end until January 1960. Almost its sole function now was to keep suspects in detention. There were 24,000 detainees in thirty-nine camps and 8,400 Mau Mau convicts in twenty-one prisons at the end of 1956. Despite a strict code of regulations, good intentions and tours of inspection by British Parliamentary delegations, a deliberately tough set of conditions, interpreted by some of the world's press as unnecessarily oppressive, existed in these camps with the intention of separating the hard-core terrorists from the mass of sympathizers. Then in 1959 the Hola Camp Scandal broke with allegations of brutality and mistreatment of detainees. However it is not the purpose of this chapter to investigate these aspects of the Emergency in Kenya. The military campaign ended in 1956. Once again the army had answered a cry for help from a colonial Governor and emerged four years later completely successful. Their success was in large measure due to the invaluable help of loyal Africans of whom over 1,800 were killed during the Emergency. The Security Forces suffered a total of 590 killed, of which only twelve were British soldiers. However 11,500 Mau Mau were killed during the struggle. The appalling casualties suffered by the Mau Mau are indicative of the fanaticism engendered by the Mau Mau movement, a fanaticism often reflected in the local security forces. Mistakes were made involving innocent persons such as the unpublicized shooting of about twenty Meru Guards after they had been mistakenly taken prisoner. One has to add that 1,015 persons were hanged for Emergency offences between October 1952 and March 1956. Yet, misplaced sympathy among British soldiers for their enemies was soon dispelled when they saw the terrible atrocities committed in the name of Freedom upon African and European Kenyans alike. Though the Kenya Campaign was not the stuff of which heroic tales are made the British Army emerged unsullied from a rather unpleasant and messy business.

6

British Guiana
1953-64

Trouble first brewed in British Guiana in October 1953. The root of the problem was the enmity between the East Indian and African communities. The East Indians – roughly 45 per cent of the population – who were brought into the colony as plantation labour after the emancipation of negro slaves in 1838, and were until 1947 disenfranchised by strict property and literacy requirements. In 1953 universal suffrage gave victory to the militantly leftist People's Progressive Party (PPP) led by Dr Cheddi Jagan. Within a few months the British Government, fearing Jagan's marked sympathy for the Communist world, found it necessary to suspend the constitution. There was some unrest in Georgetown, mostly among East Indians, and the Colonial Office decided on a precautionary move of troops to the colony. The 1st Battalion the Royal Welch Fusiliers were at the time on the Caribbean station; two companies were dispatched promptly in two Royal Naval frigates to Georgetown which they reached on 8th October. By the end of the month the 1st Battalion the Argyll and Sutherland Highlanders had arrived on board the aircraft carrier HMS *Implacable* from the United Kingdom to take over garrison duties from the Welch fusiliers who were able to return to the less arduous duties of Jamaica and Bermuda. Upon the arrival of British troops in the colony the situation immediately quietened. The Argylls were replaced by the Black Watch who, when they reached the end of their tour in 1956, were replaced not by another battalion from England but by a company from the Worcestershire Regiment who were by then

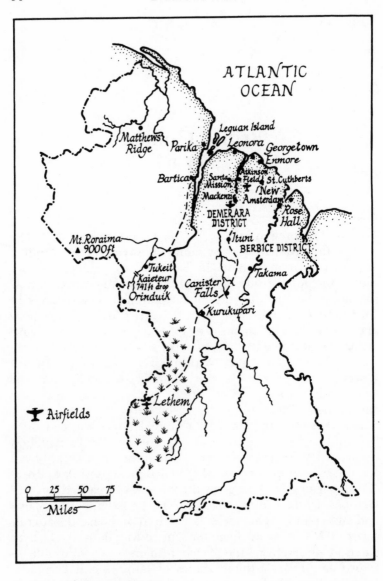

5 British Guiana 1953-64

in Jamaica.

Another election that took place in 1957 again produced a sweeping victory for the PPP. By 1961, however, Jagan's party had gained twenty of the thirty-five seats with only 43 per cent of the total vote. In February 1962 a general strike was called in protest against the budget proposed by Dr Jagan's administration. The appeal for troops was met this time by the Hampshires, who sent their battalion headquarters and one rifle company from Jamaica to join their one garrison company already *in situ*, and also by the 1st Battalion the East Anglian Regiment (the recently amalgamated Suffolks of Malayan fame and Royal Norfolks) who were flown in from England.

Spasmodic rioting had been going on for some days when on the 16th February the local police eventually appealed for military assistance. The two available companies of Hampshires were immediately committed to the fray, one to guard key installations and the other to disperse the fire-raisers and looters who by this time had set fire to a large part of what was mainly a town constructed of wood. The Hampshires adopted the well tried box formation managing to clear street after street by advancing purposefully down each one raising the standard 'Disperse or we fire' banner. Some shots were indeed fired at persistent looters but no casualties were recorded. Then quite suddenly passions subsided as quickly as they had arisen; by the end of March the only military remaining in the colony were the East Anglians.

Almost exactly a year later another general strike was staged in protest against Jagan's Government which represented almost exclusively the interests of the Asian population. The 1st Coldstream Guards had by now relieved the East Anglians who had returned to England. This time the rioting got progressively worse. At first confined to Georgetown it now spread to some of the villages south of the capital along the banks of the Demerara River. Rival factions indulged in intimidation and murder to make their point. A small patrol of the Coldstreams faced with a threatening mob that refused to disperse was forced to fire a single shot from a 7.62-mm high-velocity self-loading rifle that killed three people and wounded another. Though the intention was to employ the minimum force necessary in the circumstances much more damage than had been intended was inflicted – but such is the inevitable consequence of deploying military forces in aid of the civil power.

More troops were clearly needed. The 2nd Battalion the Green Jackets were stood by on 3rd July but the expert opinion of HQ 3 Division was that a move to British Guiana was highly unlikely. Inevitably after such emphatic assurances the order to move came at 7.45 pm that evening. The Commanding Officer, Lt-Colonel Giles Mills, who was returning by train from a briefing at Southern Command, was almost the last to know. Married men were called into barracks, equipment packed, boxes sealed and passenger manifests completed. Unbelievably six hours after the initial warning 120 men and five tons of freight left the barracks in Colchester. By Monday 8th July the battalion was concentrated in Georgetown. The strike was by now eleven weeks old and racial tension between Africans and Asians was reaching dangerous proportions. Meanwhile the Coldsteam Guards were in the process of handing over to the Grenadiers who moved into Atkinson Field and became responsible for the security of Georgetown.

The Green Jackets were deployed in various locations along the coast: A Company about twenty miles west of Georgetown across the Demerara River, C Company in Georgetown but with one platoon some seventy-five miles to the south-east and to the east of the Berbice River, and D Company about fifteen miles east of Georgetown. Their task was to provide support to the police, who were by this time extremely tired having been at full stretch for eleven weeks, and to try and prevent racial animosity from getting out of hand. They were remarkably successful; both Africans and Asians seemed delighted to see them and crowds dispersed before they had to be broken up. By demonstrating a constant military presence in the main centres of population the atmosphere of fear and distrust between the races gradually diminished. In addition to a heavy patrol programme the company commanders spoke eloquently to the village elders on the need for racial peace. Particularly adept at this was Major David Stileman. It was typical of the man, who himself had been grievously wounded in battle while serving with the Rifle Brigade in the cornfields of Normandy in 1944 and who was many times decorated for bravery, that he should speak so passionately against the need for violence.

The Green Jacket tour in British Guiana was not a particularly active or dramatic one but it serves as an example of the invaluable work done by soldiers in far-flung parts of the Empire, work for which they were not trained but work which they happily did as best they could because there often was no welfare officer, no policeman, no district officer, no doctor, no lawyer ... just a soldier to try his best to be all things to all men.

Life now became comparatively peaceful for the Green Jackets who ventured deep into the hinterland of the country out of pure curiosity rather than military necessity. The climate in British Guiana changes little throughout the year. Day and night temperature only varies between 75° and 87° F. The rainfall is heavy averaging about 10 inches per month. It is not an unpleasant climate once acclimatized but hard work for the newcomer. It was a tribute to the fitness of the battalion that the riflemen were able to stand the long patrols in the sun coming as they did straight from England.

The conference to decide the political future of British Guiana met in London on 22nd October with Mr Duncan Sandys, the then Colonial Secretary, in the chair. Elections and subsequent independence were arranged for December 1964 to be held under a system of proportional representation. A coalition of the Peoples' National Congress (PNC) led by Forbes Burnham who represented the bulk of the African community and of Peter D'Aguiar's Conservative United Force took office. Guyana today owes her independence in large measure to the patient riflemen of the Green Jackets and the soldiers of the other infantry battalions who served in the colony between 1953 and 1964. Fortunately there were no British casualties but that does not necessarily make Guyana's successful transition to independence a lesser military achievement than for instance the victory in Malaya; a different sort of operation of course but no less important.

7

Cyprus
1954-83

Cyprus was ceded to Britain in 1878 by Turkey. It remained a colony of little importance, even during the Second World War, until the British evacuation of Egypt made it the obvious choice for the site of Middle East Headquarters in June 1954. It was exactly at this juncture that the movement for Union with Greece or *Enosis*, under the leadership of Archbishop Makarios, was beginning to gain momentum. Makarios led 419,000 Greek-speaking Cypriots who shared the island with 105,000 Turks. There was little love lost between the two communities; not surprisingly the Turkish population and their sponsors on mainland Turkey were not going to agree to any form of *Enosis*.

In August 1954 the 2nd Battalion the Green Howards arrived from Egypt closely followed by the 2nd Battalion the Royal Inniskilling Fusiliers. As the military build-up associated with the siting of Middle East HQ progressed, the first stirrings of the *Enosis* movement were felt throughout Cyprus. Serious rioting in December in Nicosia and Limassol ended with British troops shooting two rioters. Meanwhile the self-styled General George Grivas, a retired Greek Army colonel, was busy setting up an army of guerillas in the mountains of Cyprus. The movement was named EOKA (Ethniki Organosis Kypriou Agonistou). The campaign can be said to have started on 1st April 1955 when a series of bombs exploded in different parts of the island. Leaflets, signed 'The Leader Dighenis', after a legendary Byzantine warrior, proclaimed that with God's help and the support of all the forces of Hellenism the struggle

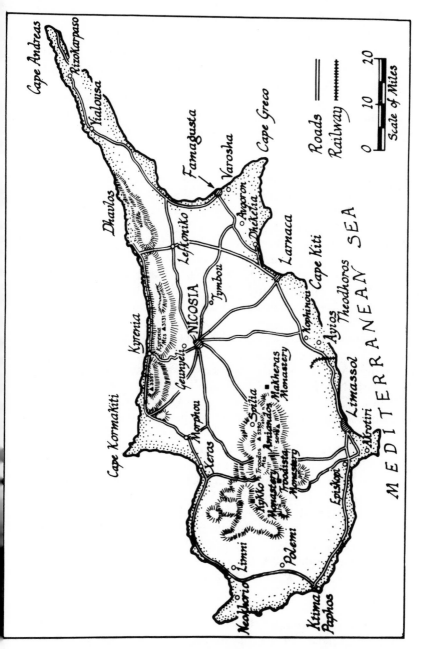

6 Cyprus: scene of operations against EOKA 1954-59 and by UN forces since 1964

to throw off the British yoke had begun. On 19th June EOKA opened its second major offensive with attacks on police stations in Kyrenia. A few days later a mountain guerilla group led by Renos Kyriakides attacked the police station in Amiandos, a small village in the massive Troodos range of mountains, and killed the sergeant in charge. Bombs were thrown in bars and in army houses all over the island. Rioting in Nicosia followed on 2nd August.

Meanwhile the new Conservative Government attempted to get a grip of the situation by inviting both the Greek and Turkish Governments to attend talks in London on the future of Cyprus. The tripartite conference opened in London on 21st August. The new Foreign Secretary, Mr Harold Macmillan, stressed the common interests of Greece, Turkey and Great Britain in the Eastern Mediterranean, particularly their membership of NATO. Macmillan made much of Britain's obligations in the Middle East, particularly the Baghdad Pact and the Treaty of Alliance with Jordan which, he said, could only be met by the possession of Cyprus. He dismissed the idea of a leased base. The talks fairly predictably ended in deadlock.

In September sixteen imprisoned EOKA terrorists escaped from Kyrenia Castle by using knotted sheets to lower themselves from a gunport to the adjacent beach. Several of these men later became terrorist group leaders. Not surprisingly public confidence in the administration was shattered. This incident and the burning of the British Institute in Metaxas Square in Nicosia on 17th September persuaded the British Government of the seriousness of the situation. On 25th September Field Marshal Sir John Harding handed over his job as Chief of the Imperial General Staff and was appointed Governor of Cyprus. He arrived on the island on 3rd October. He was closely followed by an influx of troops later the same month, namely the 1st Royal Norfolks, the 1st Gordon Highlanders, the 1st Royal Leicestershires and the 1st Battalion the Middlesex Regiment. Troops were spread throughout the island with headquarters in Nicosia, Xeros, Paphos, Limassol, Famagusta, Kyrenia, and Larnaca.

In mid November the Governor announced a £38-million development plan for the island. But it was too late. By now EOKA had gained considerable sympathy among both the clergy and the people. In late November five servicemen were killed in one week; two of these died in an ambush led by Grivas himself. On 26th November the Governor proclaimed a State of Emergency. The death penalty was extended to offences other than murder including the discharge of firearms or placing of explosives with intent to cause injury or kill. Life imprisonment was the penalty for the possession of firearms or explosives. What aroused the greatest anger amongst Cypriots was the provision made in the Emergency Regulations for collective punishment, for the whipping of youths under eighteen, deportation and censorship. The first collective punishment was imposed on 4th December at Lefkoniko after the village post office had been blown up, one of a series of incidents in the village. The Governor decided that £2,000 would be collected to pay for a new post office on the basis of a means test and that a curfew would remain in force until it was paid for. The village remained much quieter thereafter.

In furtherance of the dictum that minimum force should always be used, the army found themselves underpinning the police. Battalions therefore had to form their own riot squads armed with batons and shields and wearing steel helmets and gas masks. EOKA's aim was to pin down as many of these troops in the towns as possible to allow their guerillas more freedom of action in the hills. To this end both Athens Radio and EOKA propaganda stirred the schoolchildren of Cyprus into a frenzy of hatred against the British. On 23rd November 1955 Athens Radio described the Cypriot schoolchildren as seeing 'their fellow students persecuted and condemned to prison. But instead of hiding in their homes, they filled their pockets with stones and marched against the invaders ... it is nothing another year is wasted, what are the years worth if they are years of slavery? ... Even if many years of school are lost, even if the students remain illiterate, nothing is of value compared with the ideal which inspires them'.* As usual the soldiers maintained their patience in the face of these spitting, screaming, kicking, scratching schoolgirls. And that is to their eternal credit.

Meanwhile in the Troodos range, where the pine-covered mountains rose to over 5,000 feet, the Commandos, the Royal Scots and the Gordon Highlanders combed the hillsides for

---

* Summary of World Broadcasts, IV (BBC) 625, P7.

the EOKA gangs which operated from the villages, monasteries and caves in the area. Grivas himself had been hiding in a cave overlooking the village of Spilia. On 11th December a combined force of Royal Marine Commandos and Gordon Highlanders mounted a cordon and search operation in the area. Fortunately for Grivas his guards spotted the arrival of the British troops. Leaving behind two or three snipers under the command of one of his deputies, Renos Kyriakides, to force the British to deploy and so cause delay, Grivas himself managed to escape through thick woods. Kyriakides was wounded and captured in a gun battle with the British troops while trying to break out of the cordon near Spilia. Three Commandos were not very seriously wounded by one of their own mortar bombs. It is interesting to read Grivas' account of the action, however, in order to realize the extent to which he was removed from reality. He later wrote: 'The British believed they were surrounded and began to fire wildly in the mist and kill each other. The shooting went on for nearly half an hour; I lay flat behind a pine tree with a soldier who had been leading me on a rope. Words cannot describe what was happening. Not a branch was left on a tree. The soldiers were scattered right and left, wounded and dead. Finally one of them gave a signal and they stopped firing. Their leader had been killed: a bullet had gone through his right eye and came out at the left temple.'

On 15th December a terrorist group led by one Markos Drakos ambushed a jeep in the Troodos Mountains killing the driver. Major Coombe of the Royal Engineers who was also in the jeep jumped out and gave chase. He shot dead one of the gang, Kharalambos Mouskos, captured two others and wounded the gang leader, Drakos, who escaped. The dead terrorist was in fact a cousin of Archbishop Makarios. Inevitably the funeral in Nicosia degenerated into a riot which further exacerbated the situation. Major Coombe was awarded the George Medal. The Troodos operation had shown there were insufficient troops to cover the ground. Fortunately with the worst of the Mau Mau campaign over in Kenya there were some to spare. In January 1956 the 1st and 3rd Battalions of the Parachute Regiment were flown out from Aldershot to hutted camps in Nicosia where they formed the Island Reserve. The 1st Battalion the Royal Warwickshire Regiment arrived a few weeks later. The crisis in the secondary schools reached its climax that month. Leaflets signed by Grivas encouraged the campaign of civil disobedience. Then on 7th February a riot involving schoolchildren in Famagusta ended in tragedy. The Security Forces were forced to open fire to avoid serious injury from stoning and one of the ringleaders of the riot was fatally wounded. Harding gave schools the choice of either taking down the Greek flags they had been ordered to fly by Grivas or close down the schools. This ended the continual tussles between schoolchildren and soldiers for the Greek flags flying over the schools but, because headmasters were so severely intimidated by EOKA, effectively brought secondary education to a halt. Intimidation of elementary school staff by both EOKA and children from secondary schools also brought elementary education to a standstill so that by the spring of 1956 only eighty-one out of 499 elementary schools still functioned.

Grivas saw the closure of so many schools in Cyprus as a major achievement for EOKA. The British were portrayed as the persecutors of Cypriot schoolchildren and were powerless to influence the situation. There is no doubt that the use of children to further the aims of EOKA was both an effective and novel idea.

Meanwhile talks on the future of Cyprus dragged on between Harding and Makarios. The British offered the Cypriots self-government as soon as the security situation allowed and talks about eventual self-determination while stressing the continued importance of Cyprus as a British base. Makarios came very close to accepting the British plan but at the eleventh hour he withdrew his agreement mainly on the grounds that it offered the British the opportunity to intervene in the island's affairs indefinitely on the pretext of public security. Then on 29th February an intensive bombing campaign was started by Grivas. On 3rd March a Hermes troop transport aircraft parked on the tarmac at Nicosia Airport was blown up by a time bomb. Had it not been for a delay in the departure of the aircraft sixty-eight passengers, all soldiers and their families, would have died. Already during January and February four soldiers had been killed. Under the impression that Makarios still controlled EOKA, which in fact was no longer the case, Harding now formed the opinion that the Cypriot leader had no serious intention of coming to an agreement. He saw the renewal of violence as a breach of faith on the part of Makarios. The decision was therefore taken that, in order to resist *Enosis*, Makarios would have to be isolated. On 9th March he was arrested at Nicosia *en route* to Athens and instead was put on an aeroplane to the remote British territory of the Seychelles. On the day that Makarios was deported Harding outlined the Archbishop's close links with EOKA, his approval of the use of church funds for the purchase of arms and explosives, and the use of the archbishopric for their storage. More than anything, though, he condemned his silence while policemen, soldiers and civilians were murdered in cold blood.

Makarios' deportation coincided with a dramatic intensification of hostilities by EOKA. During the next three months there was an average of nearly two members of the security forces killed each week. The army was forced on to the defensive with the safeguarding of life and property taking priority. Inevitably offensive operations against guerillas were neglected in order to keep order in the towns. Curfew enforcement became part of the daily routine of a soldier's life. In the second half of March five British soldiers were killed and an unsuccessful attempt was made on Harding's life by a Greek Cypriot member of his staff who placed a bomb in his bed. A further dimension was added to the already complex situation by the outbreak of serious inter-communal violence sparked off, among other things, by the inclusion of Turkish policemen as legitimate targets by EOKA. On 27th April British security at Nicosia Airport was shown up for the second time in two months with the destruction of a Dakota by a bomb.

By mid-May the army had built up its strength to fifteen fighting units with the arrival of the Royal Horse Guards and the 1st Battalion the King's Own Yorkshire Light Infantry. It was now possible to revert to the offensive. A big operation was planned in the Troodos Mountains with the aim of flushing out the guerilla groups in hiding there and, if possible, eliminating Grivas himself. Two thousand troops took part in the operation, mostly Paras, Commandos and Gordons; they were aided by tracker dogs, helicopters and Auster spotter aircraft. In a series of cordon operations covering 400 square miles seventeen leading guerillas and large quantities of weapons were captured. Perhaps more important in the long term thousands of documents exposing EOKA's plans and the identities of its members were found. The mountain gangs were broken up and were no longer able to operate with impunity as they had done for so long. Grivas himself narrowly escaped capture when in the early afternoon of 11th June he and his companions, all of whom had been forced to move by the army's cordon and search operations further to the north, stopped in a wooded valley in the southern half of the Troodos range above Limassol to fill their water bottles and rest in the shade. At just this moment a patrol from the 3rd Battalion the Parachute Regiment with a tracker dog appeared below them in the bed of the stream. The six guerillas disappeared through the trees followed by a hail of fire leaving behind many of their belongings including Grivas' binoculars and spectacles. They hid up in pairs for the rest of the day in the undergrowth and Grivas effected his escape that night. It had been a close-run thing.

Despite the escape of Grivas, the operation would have been judged a considerable success had it not been for the tragic death of twenty soldiers and the serious injury of a further sixteen in a forest fire in the Paphos area. The subsequent enquiry never established whether the fire had been deliberately started by guerillas to aid their escape or whether the already very dry forest had been set alight by the army's own mortars. It was a high price to pay for the disruption of the gangs in the mountains.

The collapse of the mountain gangs was not followed by a parallel decline in violence in the rest of the island. An English schoolteacher and police officer were shot dead in June and Mr Justice Shaw was seriously wounded by gunmen. Six soldiers and eight Greeks, the latter branded as traitors or collaborators, were also killed during the same month. On 16th June EOKA threw a bomb into a restaurant and unintentionally killed the American Vice-Consul. During July and August the violence continued on the same scale with twenty-nine more soldiers, officials and Cypriots dying.

To complicate matters further Nasser seized the Suez Canal at the end of July necessitating the withdrawal of the 1st and 3rd Battalions the Parachute Regiment and the 3rd Commando Brigade to take part in the Suez landings. They

were replaced by the 1st Battalion the Oxfordshire and
Buckinghamshire Light Infantry and the Suffolks, who had so
distinguished themselves in Malaya. Two gunner regiments
were deployed in the infantry role so short were the army now
of infantry battalions. In addition three anti-aircraft regiments
were deployed in case the Egyptians decided to bomb Cyprus.

In early October a search operation codenamed
Sparrowhawk was carried out in the Kyrenia Mountains
covering about 200 square miles. While searching an isolated
farmhouse a soldier stumbled over a hole and as a result
uncovered a buried oil drum containing arms and
ammunition. The area was immediately cordoned off and in
the subsequent search a corner of corrugated iron sticking
through the pine needles gave away the location of a second
hideout containing a machine gun, ammunition, bombs,
bedding and food. Further searches of the house itself at first
proved unproductive. But perseverance paid off when the
following day an inquisitive soldier shone his torch through a
small hole in a wall behind a hanging coat, and saw a man's
head. Minutes later six men emerged through a concealed trap
door in the floor and surrendered. The gang included Pliotis
Christofi, a gang leader with £5,000 on his head; he and the
others had been hiding in a cavity between the walls which was
typical of many ingenious EOKA hideouts. All six went for
trial and were given life imprisonment for the illegal
possession of arms. The prosecution were unable to prove the
implication of the gang in an ambush in the Kyrenia Pass of a
Wiltshire Regiment convoy in which a soldier and a lady of the
WVS were killed on 28th September.

On 31st October British and French aeroplanes stationed at
RAF Akrotiri and Nicosia started bombing Egypt. Troops
normally available for internal security duties were withdrawn
to supplement the logistic effort associated with the Suez
operation. EOKA, on the defensive after the success of
Operation Sparrowhawk, regained the initiative. During
November casualties inflicted by EOKA totalled thirty-three of
which fifteen were British soldiers – the highest figure for any
comparable period during the entire emergency.

In December, however, the troops withdrawn from Suez
returned to the fray. Several guerillas were captured and
British casualties were reduced to only two. 50th Medium
Regiment who had been operating as infantrymen

demonstrated their adroitness in their new role by capturing George Raftis, leader of a guerilla group in the Paphos district, and two of his companions. A few days later another patrol driving without lights in the Paphos Forest rounded a bend and were confronted with Evaghoras Pallikarides leading two donkeys loaded with a Bren gun and other equipment. Though his companions escaped, Pallikarides, a leading EOKA terrorist, was captured. As the Security Forces' success rate increased so did the incidence of murder of those Cypriots who Grivas was convinced were betraying him. In fact many completely uninvolved Cypriots died.

In January 1957 Major-General Kendrew took over as Director of Operations combining the posts of District Commander previously held by Major-General Ricketts and Chief of Staff previously held by Brigadier Baker. 1957 started well for the Security Forces. The Suffolks shot dead Markos Drakos. The 2nd Battalion the Parachute Regiment killed or captured some fifteen terrorists during the month of January alone. In March the Duke of Wellington's Regiment killed Gregoris Afxentiou, one of the few surviving leaders of the Troodos gangs of the previous summer, near the Makheras Monastery after a grim battle in which a corporal was killed by a burst of automatic fire from the hideout in which Afxentiou was lurking. After trying every conventional method to flush Afxentiou, the soldiers surrounding the hide eventually resorted to pouring petrol down the hole and setting fire to it.

There is little doubt that at this stage the army had been spectacularly successful. During the four months ending in February the Security Forces had killed sixty-nine EOKA terrorists. Sixteen terrorist gangs had been reduced to five. Rioting and bombing had virtually stopped and most of EOKA's victims were 'soft' Cypriot targets.

Encouraged by the Greek Government, Grivas much against his will issued a cease-fire order on 14th March in which he declared he would be willing to cease hostilities if the British Government agreed to talks with Archbishop Makarios. Harding decided to acquiesce and Makarios was permitted to leave the Seychelles and return in triumph to Athens. Anglo-Greek relations improved dramatically almost overnight though relations between Greece and Turkey and the United Kingdom and Turkey took a turn for the worse. Makarios continued to sit on the fence refusing to condemn

terrorism outright. Dr Kutchuk, the leader of the Turkish
Cypriot Community, alarmed by the tendency towards
eventual self-determination, stated that the partition of the
island was the only real answer. During the summer ceasefire
EOKA rearmed and refilled its ranks but it refrained from
overt operations. The army continued to carry out low-key
operations and indeed in June came within a hair's breadth of
capturing Grivas in his hide in a house in Limassol.

The British Government now decided to try a more
conciliatory tone. As part of the new approach it was decided
to retire Harding and replace him with a colonial servant of
liberal tendencies, Sir Hugh Foot. Harding departed on 3rd
November. By the time Foot had arrived four weeks later
EOKA had blown up a Canberra bomber at Akrotiri Airfield,
an ominous foretaste of what was to come. Grivas mistrusted
Foot's motives and the Turkish community demonstrated its
disapproval of Foot's plans for self-government and eventual
self-determination by rioting in Nicosia on 27th January 1958.
The incident precipitated a pitched battle between British
soldiers and thousands of Turkish youths. Seven Turks were
killed and twelve soldiers injured. Once again the army found
itself assailed from every direction.

In late March the EOKA campaign was resumed. Fifty
bombs exploded during the first ten days of April. On 16th
April Foot asked a Greek contact to arrange for the delivery of
a personal letter from himself to Grivas in which he appealed
to the EOKA leader to suspend his campaign of violence and
sabotage to save the people of Cyprus further agony. He even
offered to meet Grivas alone and unarmed. Grivas
prevaricated; he in fact ordered a stop to the violence but,
suspecting the authorities wanted an answer to Foot's letter as
an aid to tracing him in his hideout, did not answer the letter.
On 4th May two British soldiers were shot dead as a reprisal
for alleged ill-treatment of detainees in the controversial Camp
K. Meanwhile the Turkish community, whipped into a frenzy
by broadcasts from Turkey calling for the partition of Cyprus,
campaigned vociferously for partition. Violence between the
two communities broke out in early June and reached a climax
when eight Greeks were massacred in a cornfield near the
Turkish village of Geunyeli. Once again the burden of keeping
the two communities apart fell to the British troops.

It was at this stage in the Cyprus Emergency that the

maximum number of British troops were deployed. In mid-June the 16th Parachute Brigade arrived from England followed closely by the 1st Guards Brigade, some minor units and Headquarters the 3rd Infantry Division. Although the main reason for their deployment to Cyprus was as a Middle East Reserve for possible intervention in Jordan, they were able to help with internal security duties. There were now twenty-six fighting units in Cyprus. When the 16th Para Brigade were deployed to Jordan in July, the 19th Infantry Brigade from Colchester were flown into Nicosia as replacements which was as well because violence continued to gather momentum in the island. On 17th July EOKA murdered five Turks. In desperation Foot ordered troops to make an island-wide swoop on 21st July in a last minute attempt to avert civil war. Fifty Turks and more than 1,500 Greeks were arrested. In under two months ninety-five civilians had been killed in the inter-communal violence and many more injured.

While politicians in Britain, Greece and Turkey struggled to find an acceptable answer to an insoluble problem, the British troops in Cyprus continued with their impossible task. In the north-east of the island the Welch Regiment notched up twenty-seven contacts with the enemy whilst the Royal Ulster Rifles in the Famagusta area killed three terrorists they had surrounded in a barn at the cost of one rifleman shot dead in the attack.

The assault against the army reached its worst in the summer and autumn of 1958. In August Sergeant Hammond was shot dead in Ledra Street in Nicosia, 'or Murder Mile' as the press had christened it, while walking with his two-year-old son. In October Mrs Mary Cutliffe, married to a senior NCO in the Royal Artillery and mother of five children, was shot dead while shopping in Varosha. Mrs Robinson, another sergeant's wife, was seriously wounded. This was too much even for the British Army. In less than two hours over a hundred Cypriots had been rounded up and taken to detention centres for questioning. There is little doubt that the troops were so disgusted by this horrific murder that they broke some of the rules. A thirty-seven-year-old father of six children, Panayotis Chrysostomos, was found dead with seven broken ribs at brigade headquarters. He had been arrested by the Royal Ulster Rifles in Famagusta. The subsequent enquiry found that Chrysostomos had died of heart failure while suffering from respiratory complications arising from the fracture of seven ribs. However, because the evidence of so many of the witnesses conflicted, the coroner was unable to determine how the ribs had been broken. Another Cypriot, Andreas Loukas aged nineteen, died at Karaolis Camp of severe head injuries. Again evidence was conflicting and the coroner found that Loukas had been murdered by persons unknown. An estimated 256 people were injured in the round-up. Mr Justice Trainor at Loukas's inquest commented that 'People were so assaulted and beaten that doctors were fully occupied at Karaolis Camp and the hospital tending the wounded that evening. One can fully understand the horror, disgust and anger that filled the hearts of everyone on that day but nothing can justify the assaults on persons who had done nothing to warrant them.' In the event Mrs Cutliffe's killer was never found. Although EOKA's cause was severely damaged by this appalling incident, attacks against British troops were maintained throughout the autumn and early winter. Two RAF men were killed on 11th November in a NAAFI establishment by a bomb placed by Greek Cypriot employees.

It was at this juncture that Cyprus was again discussed by the UN. The degree of accord reached at the UN between the Greek, Turkish and British representatives led to further Greek-Turkish meetings which culminated in February 1959 with the announcement in Zurich that the Greek and Turkish Prime Ministers, who had been meeting there, had reached agreement on a general plan for a settlement. Independence was now seen by all parties as the only realistic solution. *Enosis* and partition were dead. The Zurich plan provided for a Greek President and a Turkish Vice-President. Legislative authority was to be vested in a House of Representatives in a ratio of 70 per cent Greek to 30 per cent Turkish members. The judiciary, civil service, local government and the military were similarly divided. The Zurich agreement was ratified by the British Government on 19th February in London. On 1st March Archbishop Makarios was permitted to return to Cyprus. On 9th March Grivas, who had not liked much of the agreement, reluctantly ordered a ceasefire. On the 17th the guerilla leader was flown unobtrusively to Athens where he was given a hero's welcome.

As a guerilla leader Grivas was remarkably successful. He tied down 40,000 British troops and killed ninety-nine. He avoided capture in a small island for years on end. But in a wider sense he achieved very little; he perhaps brought colonial rule to an end a few years earlier than would otherwise have been the case. Suez, changing treaty obligations and longer-range and faster aircraft had made or were making Cyprus strategically redundant with or without EOKA. Nevertheless the bases were still militarily advantageous to Britain; talks to determine the status of the British bases on the island ended in July of 1960 and the way was clear for independence. Two Sovereign Base Areas (SBA) were created at Dhekalia and Akrotiri, both on the south coast of the island and covering in all some ninety-nine square miles. In addition some installations were designated 'retained sites', including the Radar station on Mount Troodos, and are still manned by the British Army or RAF whilst constitutionally they are Republican territory. On 16th August 1960 the Republic of Cyprus came into being after eighty-two years of British rule.

Sadly this was not to be the end of the story of British military involvement in Cypriot affairs. The growing antagonism and resulting violence between the two communities led eventually to intervention by a United Nations force in March 1964. The UN are still there today with the United Nations force in Cyprus (UNFICYP). The British Army has contributed an infantry battalion, an armoured-car squadron and various support elements for the past twenty years. For the most part the duties of the UN troops have been tedious and unexceptional consisting almost exclusively of monitoring, reporting, mediation and conciliation. Occasionally there have been clashes involving UN troops. One such event took place on the 15th November 1967 in the Turkish village of Kophinou which lay astride the main Episkopi–Nicosia road. For several months the Cypriot police had not been permitted to mount routine patrols in the village. On 15th November they decided to force the issue and entered Kophinou supported by elements of the Cyprus National Guard. To this day no one is quite sure who started firing, but once the first shots were heard Grivas, who had by this time returned to the island, decided to teach the Turks a lesson. He ordered the entire National Guard Battalion supported by artillery and mortars to take out the Turkish positions in Kophinou and the neighbouring village of Ayios Theodhoros.

A company of the 1st Battalion the Royal Green Jackets was

responsible for the Kophinou area, and found itself in the midst of the battle. Several platoon positions came under mortar and small-arms fire. One isolated Green Jacket section position was soon taken by a National Guard platoon. Two riflemen, still shell-shocked by two mortar-bomb explosions, were surrounded by National Guardsmen with loaded and cocked automatic weapons and were ordered to surrender their personal weapons, which they did. In the other two trenches the remaining members of the section under the command of Corporal Divine were ordered to vacate their position but refused to do so. Meanwhile in another section position commanded by Corporal Bradford equipment and clothing had been removed from tents whilst the men of the section were covered by weapons of the National Guard. The section was ordered to switch off its A41 radio set; when this was refused an officer of the National Guard, using a knife, slashed the headset. The radio operator grappled with the officer to protect his radio from further damage and the Cypriot retired with some badly cut fingers.

In all twenty-five Turkish Cypriots died during the fighting. Casualties on the Greek side were two dead and two wounded. No Green Jackets were hurt though this was more by luck than judgement. Much was made of the surrender of two weapons by British soldiers. But, in the circumstances when the riflemen were not able to defend themselves by using their weapons, the incident was hardly surprising. The Battle of Kophinou serves to illustrate the very difficult situation British troops have found themselves in on many occasions since they have formed part of UNFICYP. It is a job that requires great patience, diplomatic skill and often courage.

The National Guard inspired and executed a *coup d'état* against the Makarios Government on 15th July 1974. Makarios escaped eventually to London and one Nikos Sampson, a convicted murderer during the EOKA campaign but released as part of the amnesty on independence, was created President. This was too much for the Turks who promptly invaded and occupied the north-eastern third of the island. The *de facto* partition of the island persists to this day, even though Makarios was reinstated as President and kept the position until his death in August 1977. The Army and the RAF remain on the island both in the SBAs and as part of UNFICYP.

8

Muscat and Oman
1957-59

British involvement in Muscat dates from the early days of the
East India Company in the seventeenth century. Throughout
the nineteenth century the British and the Sultan of Muscat
found it convenient to collaborate in the suppression of piracy.
By a treaty of 1852 Britain recognized the independence of the
Sultan though, under subsequent agreements, he was able to
call on British help in time of trouble. In 1952 the Saudis
suddenly occupied the strategic oasis of Buraimi part of which
belonged to the Sheikh of Abu Dhabi, a Trucial State, and part
to the Sultan of Muscat. Ever since 1937 the Saudis had been
keen to expand their territory. The discovery of oil had given
the area a new strategic importance and provided the impetus
for the Saudis to realize a long-held ambition. The Sultan was
about to expel the invaders when the British Government
intervened and advised that the matter should be taken to
international arbitration in Geneva. But with no decision
reached by 1955 HM Government advised the Sultan to resort
to the use of force after all. The Trucial Oman Scouts (TOS), a
force recruited in the Trucial Oman States* and led by British
officers and NCOs, was imported to eject the Saudi garrison.
However during the three years it had taken to settle the
dispute, the Saudis had been busy spreading their influence in
Oman. Although historically Britain had been able to
dominate Muscat without being forced to administer the

* The former Trucial Oman States, now the Union of Arab Emirates, were
originally a British Protectorate of seven petty sheikhdoms situated to the
north and west of Muscat and Oman with which they had no political
connection.

7 Arabia: showing the relative positions of Muscat and Oman (Chapter 8), Kuwait (Chapter 9) and Aden and the Aden Protectorates (Chapter 11)

interior, the result was that now the new Imam of Oman enjoyed a large measure of autonomy. A breach between the Sultan in Muscat and Imam Ghalib Bin Ali of Oman became inevitable when a disagreement over the right to grant oil concessions was exploited by the Saudis and Radio Cairo to exacerbate relations between the two men.

In December 1955 the Sultan settled the matter by sending troops of the Muscat and Oman Field Force to occupy Nizwa, Ibri and other main centres in Oman. Under the terms of a 1920 Treaty the Sultan of Muscat was responsible for the external affairs of Oman. An oil concession, as far as he was concerned, was an external matter. However, the Sultan's success was not to last long. Ghalib, supported by his brother Talib Bin Ali and more importantly by Suleiman Bin Hamyar – Sheikh of the Beni Riyam tribe which inhabited the villages in the Jebel Akhdar – decided to resort to open rebellion. In July of 1957, while the Sultan's forces were engaged in a tactical withdrawal from Hamra to Nizwa they were repeatedly ambushed by Talib's men. They sustained heavy casualties, vehicles blew up on mines, many deserted, some fled into the desert where they died and one company was taken prisoner. The British officers with the force brought a few survivors back to Fahud, but as a fighting force it was finished. The Imam occupied Nizwa and the Sultan immediately appealed to the British for military assistance. Within a month two companies of the Cameronians were flown in from Bahrain and two squadrons of the Trucial Oman Scouts were moved into Ibri. One troop of the 15/19th Hussars was flown with their Ferret scout cars from Aden. In a very short time the opposition melted away and Nizwa was recaptured unopposed. A factor that undoubtedly helped to speed up the enemy's withdrawal was the very accurate rocket fire on the forts in the rebel town from the Venoms of the RAF, which were able to fly sorties from the RAF base at Sharjah. Ghalib, Talib and Suleiman fled with their rebel army to the Jebel Akhdar whence it was impossible to dislodge them with the forces available.

The Jebel Akhdar is one of the greatest natural fortresses in the world, a sheer limestone massif forty to fifty miles in length and twenty miles wide with peaks rising to nearly 10,000 feet. To an observer on the ground it appeared to be completely barren, but in the heart of the Jebel lay a plateau some ten

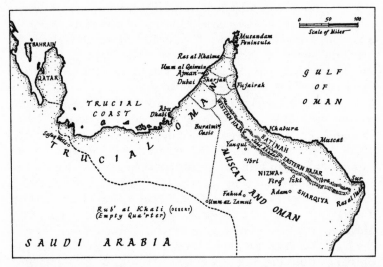

8   Muscat and Oman 1957-59: detailing the main centres of population and the Jebel Akhdar

miles wide where men have lived for centuries and where the rainfall was such that peaches and pomegranates flourished. Throughout Arabia the Jebel was believed to be impregnable, for it had never been taken. In the tenth century the Persians are reputed to have lost 9,000 men in an unsuccessful assault. The few routes that led into the Jebel were difficult to follow and easy for a defender to dominate. The three main villages on the Jebel Akhdar were Sharaijah, Saiq and Habib.

Following the events of July the Cameronians were withdrawn, perhaps unwisely, to Aden. The Sultan's army was redesignated the Sultan's Armed Forces (SAF) and a new Commander, Colonel David Smiley, seconded from the British Army. The remainder of the British contingent which was provided under the terms of an agreement drawn up between the British Government and the Sultan to expand and reorganize the indigenous military forces, consisted of a few British regular officers seconded to SAF, a handful of Marine Commandos, Royal Corps of Signals and some medical personnel. A troop of armoured cars from the 13/18th Hussars and a few RAF pilots made up a total of under fifty British servicemen of all ranks, something less than the army of 10–20,000 that Radio Cairo claimed was deployed in the

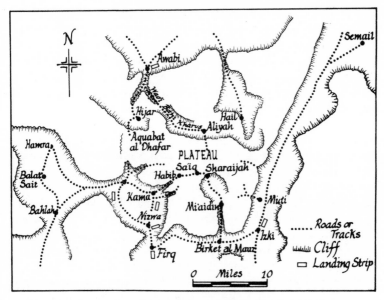

9　The area of operations during January 1959 in the Jebel Akhdar

Oman. Despite considerable success on the part of SAF in late 1957 and early 1958 in containing the rebels in the Jebel Akhdar, there could be no lasting peace while the rebels were able to operate from the safety of a secure base. Throughout 1958 an average of twenty military vehicles a month were destroyed by mines on the road between Muscat and Nizwa. Later in the year between August and December when a squadron of Life Guards had succeeded the Hussars, the new squadron managed to lose 80 per cent of their Ferret scout cars through mining though miraculously there were few casualties. Corporal-of-the-Horse Gilliland had the rare distinction of being mined on three occasions and Lt Gooch lost not only his own scout car but two others in his troop within a space of forty-eight hours. The RAF, who continuously patrolled the Jebel, reported rebel anti-aircraft fire which was subsequently confirmed to come from a ·5 Browning.

It was becoming increasingly clear to Smiley that he could not hope to capture the Jebel Akhdar with the forces he had at his disposal. In June of 1958 when Christopher Soames, the then Secretary of State for War, visited Sharjah, Smiley met him and asked for British troops to be sent to the Oman to assault the Jebel and finish matters for good. He asked for either Commandos, Paratroopers or the Special Air Service (SAS) because he felt that they were best suited to the task of assaulting a sheer rock face. In July, Smiley gleaned that 22 SAS Regiment would be returning from Malaya to England and he suggested that they might find the time to drop off for a short stay on the way home.

In mid-November the SAS arrived. D Squadron, under command of Major John Watts,* was organized into four troops or patrols of about sixteen men each. They were armed with the FN rifle, Browning machine-guns and the Energa grenade. This latter device was a high-explosive projectile designed to be fired at tanks by means of a special adapter fixed to the FN rifle. The SAS found it to be devastating when fired into caves or at buildings, preferably through windows.

Within days of their arrival the SAS were in action against the rebels. In a skirmish near Tanuf at the base of the Jebel Akhdar the SAS soldiers certainly killed one of the enemy, but they themselves had one of their best NCOs killed, shot through the heart when he showed himself on a skyline. On 1st December D Squadron led by John Watts attacked a cave occupied by the rebels. Browning machine-guns, rocket launchers and RAF Venoms supported the attack. It was not possible to close with the enemy as a 400-foot ravine separated the SAS from their quarry but it was confirmed that they had succeeded in inflicting eight casualties on the enemy without any loss to themselves. Later in December an SAS troop managed to establish itself on top of the Jebel some 2,000 yards from one of the principal rebel strongpoints, the Aquabat al Dhafar. They were accompanied by a party of some twenty dismounted Life Guards who carried nine ·5 Browning machine-guns removed from the turrets of mined Ferret scout cars. This was a remarkable feat, particularly in view of the fact that some of these men were from a recent draft fresh from their basic training at the Lifeguards Depot at Windsor. Their knowledge of infantry tactics and their experience of battle was nil. Most of them were National Servicemen. Some of the party consisted of Royal Corps of Signals, Royal Army Medical

---

* Now Major-General J.P.B. Watts CBE, MC, Commander of the Sultan of Oman's Land Forces.

Corps, and Royal Electrical and Mechanical Engineers (REME) personnel attached to the Lifeguards. This unlikely band of men was launched into the Jebel in support of the superbly professional SAS and emerged the following January as battle-hardened soldiers.

With a foothold on the Jebel secured by the Lifeguards and a platoon of local troops, the SAS mounted their attack on the Aquabat al Dhafar. Under a protective barrage from the Brownings of the Lifeguards and the mortars of the Muscat Regiment, they scaled the sheer cliffs of the Jebel with ropes and surprised the enemy in their caves. Some close-quarter fighting ensued with both sides shouting obscenities at each other in the darkness. The rebels fought stubbornly and, although once again the SAS inflicted some casualties on the rebels without loss to themselves, they maintained a healthy respect for their adversaries thereafter.

As a result of this engagement both Smiley and Watts decided that it would not be possible to take the Jebel with a single squadron of SAS. They both agreed, however, that the job could almost certainly be done with a second squadron. Government approval for a second squadron from 22 SAS Regiment was secured with the proviso that all British troops would have to be out of Muscat and Oman by April 1959. The UN were due to discuss the situation in that area at this time. Clearly Britain would be in for a rough ride if she still had troops deployed there.

On 1st January Lt-Colonel Tony Deane-Drummond, the Commanding Officer of 22 SAS, arrived in Muscat. By the 9th January a Joint Tactical Headquarters was set up at Nizwa. Its role was to co-ordinate the operations of the Sultan's Armed Forces, the SAS, the Lifeguards and the RAF. On 12th January A Squadron, 22 SAS Regiment, flew in from Malaya. It was commanded by a Major John Cooper who had been David Stirling's driver in the Western Desert in the days of the Long Range Desert Group. Cooper immediately moved his men into the area of operations both to give D Squadron a break but also in order to acclimatize his men as quickly as possible. It was now considerably colder on the Jebel, particularly at night, than the steaming heat of the Malayan jungle with which the men had become so familiar.

It was decided that on the next full moon, which was on the

night of 25th/26th January, a direct assault should be made on the Jebel by the shortest possible route and so into the heartland of the 'Green Mountain' itself – the three villages of Sharaijah, Saiq and Habib. The Aquabat al Dhafar feature was too far away from these villages and was also occupied in strength by the enemy as a result of the earlier SAS assault in that area. After comprehensive reconnaissance of the Jebel from the air, Smiley and Deane-Drummond agreed on a route up the south-western face of the Jebel just five miles north of Nizwa. There was no path as such but the route appeared to be a feasible proposition for the SAS. What was more it appeared to be unguarded.

Various diversionary moves were made to draw the enemy attention away from the chosen route. Offensive patrolling by the Trucial Oman Scouts and the SAS in the Aquabat al Dhafar area, diversionary attacks in the Tanuf and Izki areas, and false intelligence fed to the donkey drovers whose donkeys were to be used to transport stores and ammunition on to the Jebel all contributed to misleading the rebels into thinking that one of the more obvious routes on to the Jebel would be used. In fact it transpired after the attack that the rebels had reinforced their piquets on the Aquabat al Dhafar to more than a hundred strong and that both Talib and Suleiman had joined them in order to supervise the defence themselves. Most of their remaining strength was concentrated on the Tanuf track. In the event there was only one piquet guarding the route chosen by the SAS.

Due to low cloud over the Jebel the operation was postponed twenty-four hours. Then at 2100 hours on the evening of the 26th January A and D Squadrons of 22 SAS supported by the dismounted Lifeguards started the assault on the Jebel. Also involved in the operation were some tribal irregulars led by British officers; some of these were to provide support to the SAS Squadrons but the larger part, accompanied by a platoon of the Muscat Regiment, were to attempt to reach the top of the Jebel from the Awabi area to the north. At dawn air support would be provided by RAF Venoms from Sharjah and two helicopters were made available for casualty evacuation. Artillery support for the operation was provided by the 5.5-mm guns of the Sultan's forces.

About a third of the way up the side of the Jebel a stray

sniper's bullet hit and exploded a grenade in an SAS trooper's pack. He and the two men behind him were seriously wounded. Although they were evacuated by helicopter as quickly as possible, two of the three died the next day from their wounds. These were to be the only British casualties incurred during the operation. Soon after this unfortunate incident the leading SAS troopers came under ·5 Browning fire from the only piquet barring the way on to the Jebel. This was silenced within minutes by a lone SAS trooper who stalked and killed both enemy gunners with a neatly placed grenade. The SAS men then made best speed to the top. Using ropes at times and shedding equipment to climb unencumbered, the leading SAS squadron made the top of the Jebel by first light. They had taken nine and a half hours to reach their objective. The Lifeguards, close on the heels of the SAS, set up their machine-guns and secured the heights. Then exactly as planned three RAF Valettas from Bahrain dropped 30,000 lbs of equipment, ammunition, food and water to the troops on the Jebel. The Venoms which were by now making low-level runs over the plateau were, however, unable to find any targets. The opposition had mysteriously melted away. It later transpired that the supplies dropped by parachute had been mistaken for parachutists. The word soon spread the length and breadth of the Jebel that hundreds of British parachutists were descending near Habib. Without waiting to verify the truth of the rumours, the three rebel leaders decided to make good their escape.

Having secured the objective, the SAS now pressed on towards Habib and Saiq. Both were entered unopposed. Near Saiq the SAS discovered Suleiman's cave. It had clearly been very recently abandoned in a hurry. It was filled with loot, arms and ammunition as well as personal letters and documents which, when later translated, proved to be an invaluable source of intelligence. Sharaijah, the third village on the plateau, was captured the same day, although the village appeared to be almost completely deserted. The Battle of the Jebel Akhdar was over. The Sultan's authority now had to be established throughout the area. Smiley, who had arrived on the plateau by helicopter, entrusted the task of making contact with the rebels to his tribal irregulars. As the word spread that no reprisals were being taken against them, the Beni Riyam tribesmen appeared in ever-increasing numbers from the surrounding rocks and caves. Great stockpiles of arms were uncovered; these included ·5 Browning machine-guns, 81-mm and 3-inch mortars, Bren guns and American mines which carried Saudi Arabian Army markings.

Troops from the SAS, Lifeguards, TOS and SAF patrolled the Jebel Akhdar for two weeks. The area was extensively mapped and a landing strip was constructed at Saiq capable of taking twin-engined Pioneers. A company of the Northern Frontier Regiment (part of SAF) established a camp by the airstrip and a British officer attached to SAF was appointed Military Governor of the Jebel Akhdar.

Unfortunately Ghalib, Talib and Suleiman and a number of their closest followers, after moving by camel to the coast, were able to procure a dhow in which they reached the safety of Saudi Arabia. Talib, who had always been the effective leader of the rebels, retained the loyalty of a hard core of rebels who remained in Oman. They lay low for some six months after their defeat on the Jebel Akhdar but by the summer of 1959 they again were mining the roads. The mines were smuggled across the northern frontier into the Wadi Jizzi or by dhow to the Batinah Coast. Smiley realized the SAF had insufficient numbers to deal with this new threat and so obtained the Sultan's agreement to raise a paramilitary force, to be known as the Gendarmerie, to patrol both the coast and the northern frontier. Together with the SAF and the Royal Navy, the Gendarmerie managed to reduce the volume of arms smuggling, though they were never able to stop it completely. A system of rewards and reprisals also helped to get the message across. Smiley's main task, however, after the departure of the SAS for England in March and the last of the Lifeguards to Aden in May 1959, was to build up the strength of SAF. By the time Smiley left Oman in 1961 he had increased its strength to 2,000 men. Their successors still patrol Muscat and Oman today from the Wadi Jizzi in the north to Masira in the south. They still maintain an uneasy peace in a country which remains vital to Western interests. The threat today no longer comes from Saudi Arabia, with which the present Sultan maintains cordial relations, but from the Communist regime in the South Yemen Republic, formerly the British Protectorate of Aden (see Chapter 13).

The campaign in Muscat and Oman from 1957 to 1959 culminating in the spectacular assault on the Jebel Akhdar was a minor war by any standards. Very few British troops were involved and certainly they would not have been so successful had it not been for the invaluable contribution of the SAF who bore the brunt of the fighting over a much longer period. The part played by British troops was brief but devastating in its effect and is a classic example of the timely use of limited but effective military force. Between January 1958 and the end of January 1959 there were a total of seventy-three casualties. The SAF suffered eight killed and fifty-one wounded. The TOS had one British officer killed and British regiments suffered a total of six killed (three SAS, two Royal Marines and one Royal Corps of Signals) and six wounded (one SAS, three Life Guards and two Royal Marines.)

Cairo Radio reported that 120,000 British troops had been employed in the attack on the Jebel Akhdar and Moscow embellished the story still more claiming that 13,000 paratroopers had been dropped. In fact, barely 1,000 troops of which only 250 were British had smashed the myth of the Jebel Akhdar's impregnability.

9

Kuwait: A Lesson in Deterrence 1961

The Emirate of Kuwait lies at the head of the Persian Gulf squeezed between Iraq and Saudi Arabia. It covers an area of over 7,000 square miles and has a population of approximately one million. The Emirate was founded about 1700 when the harsh conditions of the interior drove the Anaiza and al-Khalifa tribes on to the coast in search of water. Water was discovered on the site of what is now Kuwait City and within fifty years the town was established as an important trading post and boat-building centre. From the early nineteenth century Great Britain developed close trading links with Kuwait; these were later threatened by Russian attempts to secure a naval supply station at the head of the Gulf. Thus in 1899 Britain acceded to Sheikh Mubarak's request for support and protection, and a treaty was concluded establishing Kuwait as an independent state under British protection. In accordance with this treaty, Kuwait's foreign relations were conducted by Britain through its political agent. In the period of post-1919 settlements the most crucial was the 1922/3 conference to settle the Kuwaiti-Saudi Arabian frontiers in which the interests of the newly established state of Iraq, under British Mandate, were also concerned. Two neutral zones were established, one of which lay between Iraq and Saudi Arabia. Thereafter fears of Iraqi expansionism were never completely eliminated. On 22nd February 1938 oil was discovered just south of Kuwait City. The Second World War delayed the full exploitation of this major new asset and it was not until 1948 that the first oil was exported by the Kuwaiti Oil Company owned jointly by British Petroleum and Gulf Oil. By 1961 Kuwait was a major oil producer and the new regime in Iraq looked with covetous eyes at its diminutive neighbour.

The Iraqi Revolution of 14th July 1958 headed by General Abdul Karim Qassim was welcomed only by the Soviet Union which hailed it as 'a great victory for the Arab national Liberation movement'. Iraq withdrew from the Baghdad Pact and abrogated the 1955 Anglo-Iraqi agreement in March 1959; in May 1959 the last British soldiers left Iraq. The Iraqi Ba'ath movement which Qassim headed was dedicated to the overthrow of all Western-oriented conservative régimes in the region, particularly Kuwait to which Iraq had traditionally laid claim. On 19th June 1961 an exchange of notes between Britain's Political Resident in Kuwait and Sheikh Abdullah As-Salim As Sabah, who had succeeded as ruler of Kuwait in 1950, terminated the 1899 agreement and Kuwait became an independent state, though clause 4 of the note provided for British assistance if such assistance was requested by the Kuwait Government.

On 25th June President Qassim renewed the claim that Kuwait was part of Iraqi territory and that he intended to annex it forthwith. The Emir of Kuwait immediately appealed to both Great Britain and Saudi Arabia for aid. The new Middle East Command had been set up the previous March in Aden and Air Marshal Sir Charles Elsworthy created C-in-C. It replaced HQ British Forces Arabian Peninsula which had been the brainchild of Templer in 1958. The new Headquarters was a demonstration of Britain's intention to be able to intervene anywhere in the Middle East in defence of her own or her allies' interests. The system was tested perhaps more quickly than had been expected. Intelligence reported that Iraq was not bluffing and was indeed assembling an armoured force close to the Kuwait border. The British Government headed by Harold Macmillan, mindful of its treaty obligations to Kuwait but also extremely sensitive to any threat to British oil interests in the Gulf, ordered Elsworthy to put sufficient forces into Kuwait immediately to deter any aggression by Iraq.

42 Commando were by coincidence *en route* from the Far East in the Commando carrier *Bulwark*. Making best possible speed she managed to arrive off Kuwait on the morning of 1st July. The Commandos went ashore and secured the aerodrome which allowed a squadron of Hunters to land hours later. 42 Commando were quickly followed by elements of 45

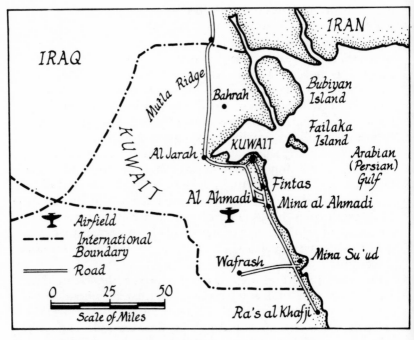

10   Kuwait: showing the Mutla Ridge

Commando from Aden and two companies of the 2nd
Battalion the Coldstream Guards, who were at the time on
detachment at Bahrain from Kenya. The infantry were joined
by two troops of Centurion tanks manned by men of the
Carabiniers who were landed on the Kuwait shore from the
Tank Landing Ship HMS *Striker*. Thus by nightfall on 1st July a
weak brigade with air support had been rushed to Kuwait to
counter the Iraqi threat. This was no mean achievement. The
build-up continued the following day so that the remainder of
45 Commando, a battery of the 33rd Para Field Regiment and
A Squadron of the 11th Hussars with Ferret scout cars had
arrived by the evening of the 2nd July. On 3rd July the 11th
Hussars set out for the border with Iraq which they patrolled
without seeing any sign of the enemy. The same day the
remainder of the Carabinier squadron took over the Centurion
tanks that had been stockpiled in Kuwait for just such an
eventuality as this and the 2nd Battalion the Parachute
Regiment flew in from Cyprus slightly delayed by a ban on

overflying by Turkey. They brought with them their long-range wire-guided Malkara anti-tank guided missiles mounted on Hornet vehicles. Malkara packed a tremendous punch and was more than a match for Iraq's Soviet-supplied tanks. The entire force was commanded by Brigadier D.G.T. Horsford.

An appreciation of the ground quickly showed that the vital ground that had to be occupied if an Iraqi thrust was to be held and defeated was a feature called the Mutla Ridge. This was some twenty-five miles from the airfield which the British troops now occupied and sufficiently close to the border to prevent any meaningful occupation of Kuwaiti territory. The day after their arrival the British were ferried out to their positions by means of requisitioned transport and immediately started to dig defensive positions. Digging proved difficult and for the most part sangars were constructed. These were constructed with rocks and stones and provided cover from small-arms fire.

The heat in July in Kuwait is almost unbearable for a European. The temperature rises to 125° Fahrenheit at midday. On the Mutla Ridge there was no relief from the searing rays of the sun. It was possible to fry an egg on the hull of a Centurion tank if the egg had not already hard boiled in the sun and the troops made instant coffee with water straight from the jerrican. For the soldiers to survive the day it was necessary for them to drink at least two gallons of water – and water resupply was a major problem for the first few days. However Horsford soon enlisted the aid of the Kuwaiti Oil Company who loaded water and ice on to Royal Naval helicopters at Al Ahmadi and had it flown up to the Mutla Ridge. Much was made in the British Press of the incidence of heat exhaustion among the troops but at no time was the force so depleted that it was incapable of battle – as some newspapers suggested. The quickest way of getting those soldiers that did collapse from heat exhaustion back on their feet was to evacuate them by helicopter to air-conditioned quarters in Kuwait City or Al Ahmadi where they normally recovered within twenty-four hours.

On 4th July the 1st Battalion the Royal Inniskilling Fusiliers and 34 Squadron Royal Engineers arrived from Kenya and two days later they were followed by the 1st Battalion the King's

(Manchester and Liverpool) Regiment. The rest of the Carabiniers arrived with more tanks and the 7th Para Field Regiment, Royal Artillery from Aldershot provided much-needed artillery support. 42 and 45 Commando were both relieved on the Mutla Ridge and returned to the *Bulwark*.

Horsford's men now played a waiting game in the Kuwait desert. Meanwhile the Macmillan Government brought pressure to bear on friendly Arab states to help shoulder the burden. By September the Arab League managed to muster sufficient forces to take over the protection of Kuwait from Great Britain. The Paras were the first to go and by 19th October the British withdrawal was complete.

Although not a shot was fired in anger the British troops by their very presence prevented an almost certain invasion of Kuwait by Iraq but more important demonstrated the resolve of the British Government to go to the aid of an ally and to protect vital British interests with force if need be.

10

Brunei and Borneo
1962-66

Approximately three-quarters of the island of Borneo forms part of the Republic of Indonesia whilst the remaining quarter along the northern coast of the island was in 1962 under British colonial rule or protection. In the north-east was the colony of North Borneo or Sabah; to the west lay the Sultanate of Brunei and stretching along the remainder of the northern coast was the colony of Sarawak. Indonesian Borneo, otherwise known as Kalimantan, had for centuries been administered by the Dutch and it formed an important part of the Dutch East Indies until Indonesia achieved independence in 1949. Sukarno, Indonesia's first President, had since 1945 dreamed of bringing the Malay Peninsula, Singapore, Sarawak, Sabah and Brunei under the domination of a Greater Indonesia.

The man who most stood in Sukarno's way was Tunku Abdul Rahman, Prime Minister of the Malayan Federation since the country gained its independence from Britain in 1957. The Tunku soon realized that the only way to live with his giant neighbour to the south was to create a large and, in his view, a more viable political unit consisting of the Federation of Malaya, Singapore, and the British colonies of Sarawak and Sabah and the Sultanate of Brunei. The Tunku made his first formal reference to 'Malaysia' on 27th May 1961 whilst speaking to the Foreign Correspondents' Association of South-east Asia in Kuala Lumpur. The idea soon gathered momentum: only the Sultan of Brunei hesitated. It was here in Brunei that Sukarno saw his chance to foment trouble. On 8th December 1962 the North Kalimantan National Army led by

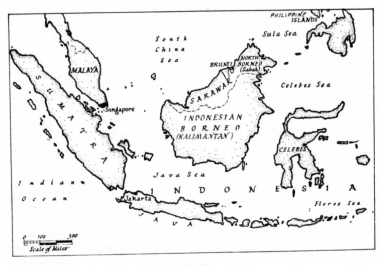

11 South-East Asia (Chapters 3 and 10)

an absentee politician, A.M. Azahari, a 34-year-old Arab-Malay, rose in revolt against the Sultan who immediately requested help from the British Government. A force of British and Gurkha troops were quickly dispatched by air and sea from their bases in Singapore. On 16th December British Far Eastern Command issued a statement saying that all major centres in Brunei had been cleared of the rebels. On 19th December Major-General Walter Walker, who had established a considerable reputation as an expert in jungle warfare during the Malayan emergency, was appointed Commander British Forces Borneo Territories.

It was not until the following May that the last of the rebels in Brunei were eliminated. Whilst British troops dealt with the last spasms of the Brunei revolt, Jakarta Radio broadcast a series of inflammatory statements designed to increase tension in Borneo. On 20th January 1963 the Indonesian Foreign Minister, Dr Sabandrio, announced a policy of 'confrontation' towards Malaya 'because at present they represent themselves as accomplices of neo-colonialist and neo-imperialist forces pursuing a policy hostile towards Indonesia'. The war of words dragged on interspersed with various attempts at reaching a political understanding, though how genuine these attempts were on the part of Indonesia is open to some doubt since groups of Indonesian 'volunteers' had begun in April to infiltrate across the border into Sarawak and Sabah where they engaged in raids, sabotage and attempted subversion. On 27th July President Sukarno stated that 'to crush Malaysia we must launch a confrontation in all fields. We cannot talk sweetly to the imperialists'. Then on 16th August a Gurkha Rifles unit clashed with what a British Army spokesman at the time called 'a group of about fifty Indonesian-based terrorists' on the Sarawak border. On 16th September 1963 the Federation of Malaysia formally came into being with only Brunei choosing to opt out. Indonesia promptly broke off diplomatic relations with Malaysia. Two days later the British Embassy was burned by a mob of 10,000 in Jakarta. The scene was set for what was almost certainly Britain's last jungle war.

When General Walter Walker arrived in Borneo in December 1962 it was to a country with few motorable roads outside the urban areas and no railways. There was only one deep-sea port at Labuan. Initially there were no stockpiles of military supplies; they would have to be brought in some 900 miles from Singapore by sea and air. There were no camps for the troops, no generators, no pumping engines, no workshops and no local military forces from which to obtain advice or assistance. General Walker's first task was therefore to create the military infrastructure which would allow him to build up his forces to meet the Indonesian threat. In December 1962 his forces consisted of one infantry brigade of three battalions, six naval coastal minesweepers and some fifteen naval and Air Force helicopters. When he handed over command in March 1965 there was a multi-national force in Borneo consisting of some 18,000 men of which over half were British and the remainder were Gurkha, Malay, Australian or New Zealanders. There were some 1,500 border scouts recruited from the indigenous tribes – Dyak, Sea Dyak, Kenyan, Keyan and half a dozen others. In addition there was a considerable naval presence of coastal minesweepers and fast patrol boats, some eighty helicopters and about forty fixed-wing aircraft which included delta-wing Javelin fighters. Walker's force also included a composite regiment of the Special Air Service Regiment (SAS), the squadrons being British, Australian and New Zealand, and two regiments each of armoured cars, engineers and artillery.

12   North Borneo: showing the five administrative 'divisions' into which
British Borneo was divided

At first sight the strategic problem of defending Malaysia
from outside aggression must have seemed insurmountable.
Half of the Federation lies hundreds of miles away making
redeployment and reinforcements more than usually difficult.
The 900-mile land border with Indonesian Borneo is covered
in dense rain forest. All the Malay Peninsula can be reached by
canoe from Sumatra. The island of Borneo is set at the very
centre of the Indonesian Archipelago and forms the southern
limit of the South China Sea. It is about 850 miles in length
and 600 miles across at its greatest width. The equator cuts
across the centre of the island making the climate inhospitable
in the extreme. Vast mountain ranges dominate the island
interspersed with valleys and plateaus all of which are covered
by tropical rain forest. The jungle is as daunting as anything
that British troops met in the Malayan emergency or the war in
Burma. The 100-foot trees cast a deep green gloom. The
streams are infested with leeches. The hillsides are sometimes
almost vertical. A pair of canvas jungle boots rots after two
weeks. In the lowland swamp areas of Western Borneo the
nights are nearly as hot as the days. Elsewhere in the highlands,
the night air is so cold that mens shiver in their jungle-green
uniforms even inside a sleeping bag.

The first test came on 28th September 1963 when about 200

Indonesian raiders crossed the mountains into the jungles of the Third Division and launched an attack on the small outpost at Long Jawai. The garrison there consisted of six Gurkha soldiers, three policemen and twenty-one Border Scouts. Despite a spirited defence Long Jawai fell. The Indonesians had scored their first major success. However, the distance that the Indonesian force had penetrated, some fifty miles, was their downfall. They had to get back to the border on foot. Wessex helicopters of 845 Squadron, Fleet Air Arm, flew platoons of the 1/2nd Gurkha Rifles into ambush positions along the intruders' likely line of retreat. A large proportion of the Indonesian force was destroyed in several actions over the next twelve days including twenty-six Indonesians who were killed instantly when their two longboats were expertly ambushed by a platoon of Gurkhas in position on the river-bank.

During the next three months there were several minor incidents spread along the entire length of the frontier. Then in the last three days of 1963 a strong force of raiders, which included some thirty-five regular soldiers, crossed the border near Tawau on the north-east coast of Sabah. Their aim was to capture the village of Kalabatan thirty miles west of Tawau. The half-company of the 3rd Royal Malay Regiment in Kalabatan was taken completely by surprise when the Indonesians attacked just before midnight killing the company commander and seven soldiers and wounding nineteen others. Walker hurriedly called in the 1/10th Gurkha Rifles and, employing the same tactics he had used so successfully after Long Jawai in September, he used helicopters to cut off the intruders' line of retreat. Within a month only six of the original Indonesian force had not been killed or captured by the Security Forces – a remarkable military achievement.

In January 1964 a small patrol of the 1st Battalion the Royal Leicestershire Regiment attacked an Indonesian encampment astride the Sarawak-Sabah border. The Indonesians fled leaving seven dead and large quantities of arms and ammunition. The track record for Sukarno had not been too good to date and, to give himself a breathing space, he called a ceasefire. Predictably negotiations broke down after a month. In March the Indonesians resumed operations but with a difference. The control of operations now passed to the

Indonesian Army and Commonwealth troops started to take on units of regular Indonesian soldiers rather than bands of irregular volunteers stiffened by a proportion of regular army advisers. The 2/10th Gurkhas were the first to clash with a regular unit of the Indonesian Army on 7th March in a treacherous area astride the border ridge in Sarawak's 2nd Division. In the initial action two Gurkha soldiers were killed while approaching the Indonesian position situated on a pinnacle. After a sharp fight the Indonesians withdrew leaving one dead man on the position. Intelligence later confirmed he had been one of forty regulars of 328 Raider Battalion. Some days later the Indonesians returned to the ridge but some sixteen miles to the east. This time they were engaged by two Wessex helicopters firing SS11 anti-tank guided missiles, a troop of 105-mm light guns and two Saladin Armoured Cars. Even with this fire support, the Gurkhas had to fight hard to dislodge the Indonesians who left two dead soldiers behind when they withdrew.

The same pattern of company-sized attacks by regular units continued until September. Even with the help of helicopters the British and Malaysian forces found it increasingly hard to cope as more and more enemy bases were established just over the border in Kalimantan. It soon became apparent that these bases would have to be destroyed or at least pushed back from the border if ever a lasting solution to the war was going to be found. The situation was further complicated when on 2nd September Sukarno decided to take the war to the Malayan mainland. Parachute landings were made near Labis in Johore. Other groups managed to slip undetected across the Malacca Straits and land on the west coast. However all the intruders were rounded up remarkably quickly due almost entirely to the fact that the local support they had been briefed to expect did not materialize. Although the operation was a complete failure the invaders did manage to tie down badly needed reinforcements for Borneo.

But the initiative was soon to change hands. Under pressure from Walker, the British Government agreed to a limited number of cross-border operations into Kalimantan. These operations were usually conducted in company strength and only undertaken within the range of artillery support, at that time out to about 18,000 yards. They were always aimed at known Indonesian bases which had been reconnoitred by SAS patrols. The degree of force used in these attacks was designed not to escalate hostilities, merely to induce the Indonesians to move their bases back from the border. Each British success was euphemistically described in a press release as 'a successful action in the border area'. The fact that these attacks were kept secret until very recently is really quite remarkable. Sukarno was prepared to accept small-scale defeats in silence but clearly he would not have suffered in the same silence had the British mounted large-scale attacks.

By January 1965 a variety of new weapons had been issued to the British troops in Borneo. These included the American 5.65-mm calibre high-velocity Armalite rifle, which was much more suited to jungle warfare than the much heavier 7.62-mm self-loading rifle (SLR) issued to the British Army in the late 1950s for use in the European theatre. The General-Purpose Machine-Gun (GPMG) replaced both the Vickers Medium Machine-Gun and the Bren Light Machine-Gun, though most units continued to use the Bren on patrol because it was so much lighter and more manageable. The old 3-inch mortar was replaced by the much more effective 81-mm mortar and the 3.5-inch Rocket Launcher by the Swedish-designed 84-mm Carl Gustav medium anti-tank weapon, used in Borneo against boats and buildings. Most deadly of all was the American electrically detonated Claymore mine, which stood on four small legs and blew its lethal content of 900 ball bearings laterally out to an effective range of about seventy-five yards and over a wide arc. It proved to be a highly effective ambush weapon, so much so that a small four-man patrol could set up an exclusively 'Claymore ambush' covering up to a hundred yards of jungle track and so taking on perhaps thirty or forty men in an instant. Tobias seismic detectors completed the picture and enabled the jungle 'forts' sited by the British along the length of the border, but a mile or two back from it, to establish remote listening posts some distance from their perimeters. This network of platoon and company-sized forts was strengthened and improved as the undeclared war continued into 1965. They were usually built on high ground and surrounded by a perimeter of barbed wire and 'punjis' – sturdy fire-hardened bamboo sticks sharpened at both ends and driven into the ground at the appropriate angle so as to present a would-be attacker with an array of needle-sharp bamboos at thigh height upon which it was hoped he would impale himself. A trench and bunker system allowed the defenders to man the perimeter in comparative safety. The ground for perhaps a hundred yards from the perimeter was cleared to create effective fields of fire. Each base had its own indigenous 81-mm mortar or 105-mm howitzer support or both and bases were if possible sited to permit artillery fire support from a neighbouring unit. To complete a comprehensive defensive system, Claymore mines were sited to provide an electrically detonated explosive barrier around the fort.

The jungle forts were not built to implement a static defensive posture but to serve as bases from which aggressive patrolling could take place along the border, over the border and in the rear areas, where it was equally important to win over the hearts and minds of the local people. Reserve platoons were located further back from the border at battalion headquarters which was usually accessible by a motorable road of sorts. Life was a considerable strain for soldiers in the forward bases along the border and it was important that they should be relieved on a regular basis. Usually a platoon was sent back to battalion headquarters at least once in a six-month tour for a period of several weeks. There they would wallow in the luxury of sleeping on a bed, however basic, and having a daily shower, however primitive the plumbing.

Rest periods in the rear area seemed comparatively short-lived. Soldiers spent most of a six-month tour operating from the forward company bases. Ten to twelve-day patrols were the norm with perhaps three or four days as guard platoon in the company base before the next patrol. These brief respites between patrols were spent recovering from the effects of the previous patrol: getting rid of the grime and dirt, removing a ten-day growth of beard – sweet-smelling shaving preparations would have been guaranteed to give away a patrol's position – drawing new clothing and equipment and cleaning and checking personal weapons for the next patrol. Letters and parcels, delivered by helicopter or parachute to company bases, were gratefully received and answers were lovingly and laboriously written well into the night. 'Girlie' magazines did the rounds as each man endeavoured to commit to memory the image of the large-breasted blonde who adorned the centre pages. Somehow the bare-breasted Dyak women in the surrounding kampongs were not quite the same. Re-equipped and refreshed, platoons went back on patrol and quickly resumed their jungle routine.

Patrolling in Borneo was a strain. There was always a likelihood of an encounter with the enemy, though when it happened it was often unplanned, unexpected and fleeting in nature. Whether the instigator or the victim of an ambush, contact with the enemy was often over in seconds. The ability to shoot quickly and accurately was undoubtedly the most important requirement in the jungle, a requirement made more difficult by the fact that a few minutes or even seconds of action was almost certainly preceded by weeks, even months without contact with the enemy, a situation guaranteed to dull the senses and deaden the mind. The perpetual dilemma of a patrol commander was whether to follow a track and risk walking into an ambush or treading on an anti-personnel mine or to hack his way through nearly impenetrable secondary jungle at the rate of perhaps 200 yards an hour. Inevitably risks had to be taken or the jungle could never have been dominated. Tracks were used in order to get to the border area or beyond it in order to ambush tracks that it was hoped the Indonesians would use. It was a game of cat and mouse, of hide and seek and sometimes even of bluff and counter-bluff.

At five o'clock it started to get dark as the jungle canopy filtered out the light. Patrols broke track and established a bivouac area for the night, movement after dark in the jungle without artificial light being considered impracticable. A circular perimeter was established, sentries posted, and a cold evening meal quietly eaten. For most of the campaign in Borneo it was considered unsafe to cook in the jungle as the resultant aroma could reveal a platoon's position. At six o'clock – on the dot in the monsoon season – it started to rain. The jungle rain takes an hour to come through the trees then it goes on dripping long after the storm itself has stopped. Often it fell steadily for five or six hours seeping through holes in the soldiers' lightweight shelters and turning the jungle floor to mud. Men slept in boots and jungle-green uniforms unshaven and unwashed. The nights were terribly long – a full twelve hours between dusk and dawn. Even the exhaustion caused by the previous day's march could not fill those hours with sleep.

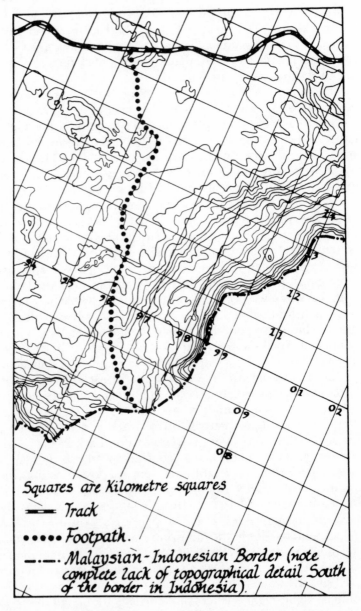

Squares are Kilometre squares

═══ Track

•••• Footpath.

—·—· Malaysian-Indonesian Border (note
complete lack of topographical detail South
of the border in Indonesia).

13   Map showing part of the border region in the First Division (Sarawak).
This map was used by the author on operations in Borneo. Lack of contours
and other topographical detail in Indonesia made navigation difficult

Men lay awake thinking of sex or the cold tin of NAAFI beer waiting at the end of the patrol.

Despite General Walker's new offensive policy and the improving quality of his soldiers' equipment, the Indonesians mounted their most ambitious venture of the entire Borneo campaign early in the morning of 27th April 1965. They attacked the company base at Plaman Mapu in the First Division. It was held by Company Headquarters and a weak platoon of B Company of the 2nd Parachute Regiment. The assault began in the pre-dawn gloom and was supported by light mortars and rocket launchers. The attacking Indonesian force rushed the thinly defended perimeter and managed to establish a small foothold inside the barbed-wire defences. There followed some close-quarter combat in which both sides fought with great courage; at one stage the British Company Segeant-Major grabbed a machine-gun from a wounded paratrooper and rallied his men by standing up and emptying a magazine of ammunition into the enemy at almost point-blank range. Only with difficulty and after an hour and a half's vicious fighting did the paratroopers manage to eject the Indonesians from their position. The Parachute Regiment lost two killed and eight wounded in the action but inflicted approximately thirty casualties on the enemy. The battle at Plaman Mapu showed that the Indonesian Regulars were well equipped and that they were able to fight with courage and determination.

The Parachute Regiment aided by the Argyll and Sutherland Highlanders and supported by Australian artillery hit back at the Indonesians in May and June of 1965 in a series of actions in which the British units killed or wounded about forty-six Indonesians for the loss of only one paratrooper killed and one Argyll wounded. After Plaman Mapu Major-General George Lea, the new Director of Operations, stepped up cross-border operations in an attempt to dominate the border area and an area beyond deep into Kalimantan. In this aim he was largely successful. The 1/2nd, the 2/2nd, the 2/6th and the 2/7th Gurkhas were all involved in clashes along the length of the Sarawak border and in the area of the junction of the Sabah and Sarawak borders, a sector that included part of Brunei as well. The Scots Guards and the 2nd and 3rd Green Jackets were all involved in successful actions in the First

Division in the latter half of 1965. The 2nd Green Jackets claimed forty-three enemy dead for the loss of only one rifleman. The 3rd Green Jackets who, unlike their 2nd Battalion, only completed one tour in Borneo, were credited with eight Indonesian dead and five wounded. The First Division area of responsibility now quietened considerably and the 3rd Green Jackets, who were there until January 1966, returned time and time again from patrols having seen little or nothing of the enemy who had virtually abandoned all offensive action.

It was on one of General Lea's cross-border operations that Lance-Corporal Rambahadur Limbu of the 2/10th Gurkha Rifles won the Victoria Cross. The exact location of this action has still not been made public but it is known to have been 'in the border area' in the First Division near Bau. On 21st November a group of Indonesians were located digging a company defensive position on top of a sheer-sided hill. C Company, commanded by Captain Maunsell, was ordered to find and destroy the Indonesian position. After three days of meticulous reconnaissance Maunsell made his plan of attack. He personally led his company to within ten yards of the enemy position along a tunnel of secondary jungle which his leading scouts had cut out with a pair of secateurs! Then an Indonesian sentry saw some movement and unslung his rifle – he was promptly shot dead by one of the Gurkha lead scouts. There was now no alternative but to assault the position immediately. Speed was essential. The Gurkhas rushed up the ridge hurling grenades and firing from the hip. One Gurkha was killed instantly by a hail of machine-gun fire while another was wounded. On the other flank Lance-Corporal Rambahadur Limbu moved with his Bren-gun team to silence a troublesome machine-gun. In the ensuing fight both members of his gun team were killed. Rambahadur was convinced they were still alive and, springing to his feet, he ran across open ground while heavy machine-gun fire kicked up the dirt around his feet and carried the first of his fallen comrades to the safety of a hut that the Gurkhas had occupied. He then retraced his footsteps and carried the other man to safety. That he was not hit by the very persistent machine-gun fire was extraordinary. The cruellest blow of all was that both the men Rambahadur had rescued were already dead.

Amazingly Rambahadur risked his life again to collect his team's Bren gun which was lying in a trench on a flank of the Indonesian position. As if immune from the deadly fire sweeping across the open ground, Rambahadur reached his gun and proceeded to launch a lone attack on the Indonesian machine-gun trenches, which he quickly put out of action. He personally killed four Indonesians.

After an hour's hard fighting with rifle, grenade and bayonet the Gurkhas ejected the Indonesians from the ridge killing twenty-four of them. They then repulsed three major counter-attacks with the aid of artillery support. During one of these Corporal Krishabahdur Rai fired a 150-round burst from his GPMG into the gathering Indonesians putting them to flight single-handed and causing many casualties. Captain Maunsell, having achieved his mission, then ordered his men to withdraw. Their move out was severely complicated by having to carry their three dead and one seriously wounded soldier. As soon as he was clear, Maunsell brought down a barrage of artillery fire on the Indonesian position. The battle had lasted about ninety minutes.

Maunsell and one of his platoon commanders were awarded the MC and Rambahadur the VC. His citation stated that he had 'displayed heroism, self-sacrifice and devotion to duty and to his men of the very highest order. His actions on this day reached a zenith of determined, premeditated valour which must count among the most notable on record'.

The rest of 1965 was comparatively quiet. Perhaps the worst menace was the widespread use of simple wooden 'cigar-box' anti-personnel mines laid by raiders along the border tracks. A number of legs and feet were lost. It introduced a macabre and sickly note into patrolling. The regiments continued to come and go: the Scots Guards, the King's Own Scottish Borderers, the Gordons, the Durham Light Infantry, the Commandos. Then in March 1966 the 1/10th Gurkhas who had taken the Bau district over from the 2/10th, scored a brilliant success killing thirty-seven Indonesians in a classically executed ambush suffering no loss themselves. This was strangely not only the most spectacular success of the campaign but also by coincidence virtually the last.

Sukarno's position in Indonesia had been seriously undermined after his flirtation with the Communist Party; he was reduced to the status of a puppet president while General Suharto took over effective leadership of the nation in March 1966. Peace feelers were put out which culminated in the signing of an agreement in Jakarta on 11th August 1966. Hostilities continued in a small way right up to the signing of the peace agreement. In mid-July the Queen's Own Buffs had taken over the Serian sector of the First Division and so became the fifteenth British infantry battalion to serve in Borneo. The brunt undoubtedly had been borne by the eight Gurkha battalions and the two Royal Marine Commandos. The Gurkhas suffered forty-three killed and eighty-seven wounded, the Commandos sixteen killed and twenty wounded and the British battalions sixteen killed and fifty-one wounded. Total Commonwealth losses were 114 killed and 180 wounded. Officially Indonesian casualties were put at 600 killed but it is certain that they were considerably greater as a result of the British cross-border operations. In terms of casualties it was a very minor war but for both the Malaysians and the British too much was at stake – the future of Malaysia and the continuation of British influence in the area – to take the matter at all lightly. The Borneo campaign must rank as one of the British Army's tidiest post-war achievements. It could have so easily developed into an endless entanglement in a frustrating jungle war. In the event a brave, if not well led, enemy was soundly defeated without bravado and self-congratulation in three years and nine months. Mr Denis Healey, the then Minister of Defence, declared in the House of Commons that the Borneo campaign would be recorded 'in the history books ... as one of the most efficient uses of military force in the history of the world'.

16 View of the SAS approach route onto the Jebel Akhdar, Muscat and Oman 26th January 1959

17 Men of 42 Commando Royal Marines camouflage their vehicles on the Mutla Ridge, Kuwait

18 Supplies being dropped to a Borneo jungle base, May 1965

19 Royal Marine Commandos on river patrol near the border with Indonesia

20 Paratroopers of the 3rd Battalion on patrol in the Radfan, May 1964

21 Paras and Commandos on patrol together in Aden town

22 Paras resting after capturing a rebel stronghold in the Radfan

23 Arab suspects arrested following a fire at a Public Works Department fuel depot in Aden, February 1967

24 British troops face a mob in the Falls Road area of Belfast

25 A Ferret armoured car on patrol in Londonderry

26 Soldier of the 7 Para Royal Horse Artillery in Belfast

27 Guerillas operating from the Yemen fire mortar shells at the SAF base of Sarfeit, October 1975

28 British troops in thickly wooded country in the Jebel Qara, behind Salalah, on the south coast of Dhofar. The monsoon weather makes this the only green place in South Arabia

29 A guerilla unit on operations in the Dhofar mountains, October 1975

30 SAS troopers assault the Iranian Embassy, May 1980

11

South Arabia
1964-67

1. Radfan

The British Government realized that they had something more than a tribal uprising on their hands when, on the morning of 10th December 1963, a grenade was thrown at the British High Commissioner, Sir Kennedy Trevaskis, and several Ministers of the Federation of South Arabia who were gathered together on the tarmac of Aden Civil Airport waiting to fly to London for a constitutional conference. In the ensuing explosion the High Commissioner's Assistant, George Henderson, and an Indian woman were killed and fifty-three people, including Sir Kennedy Trevaskis and a number of British and Federal officials, were wounded. The explosion marked the beginning of a campaign of appalling violence and bloodshed.

Aden went unnoticed in the scramble for Empire until the introduction of the steamship in the early nineteenth century. In 1839 the Aden Peninsula was acquired as a coaling station on the route to India by the East India Company from the Sultan of Lahej in return for a sizeable annual pension. From the start Aden was regarded as an adjunct to India. It became in fact a dependency of the Government of India and remained as such until it became a Crown Colony in 1937. Inland from Aden was the Sultanate of Lahej and a disparate collection of emirates and sheikhdoms. No serious attempt was made by the British to control the hinterland beyond Aden itself until after

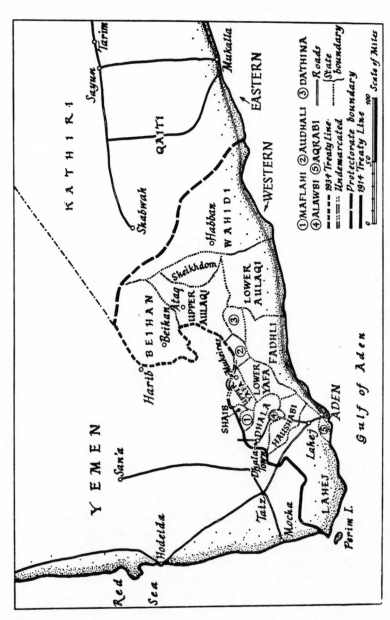

14   The Aden Protectorates

the Turkish invasion of Yemen and the territories surrounding Aden in the 1870s. The Turks were repulsed with British military aid. After this it was not difficult to persuade the local rulers to accept British 'protection'. Thus was formed over the ensuing years the Western Aden Protectorate comprising eighteen tribal territories immediately adjacent to and to the north-east of Aden and the Eastern Aden Protectorate consisting of three larger territories much farther to the east. Although Britain became responsible for the defence and foreign relations of the Protectorates, the internal administration of the various parts of the territory was entirely a matter for the indigenous rulers. Aden, on the other hand, after 1937 enjoyed the full status of a Crown Colony.

This state of affairs continued, except for occasional rumblings, until the 1950s. Inter-tribal ructions and rivalries had been a matter of normal form over the years. It was not until 1955, when two RAF officers and several Aden Protectorate Levies – members of a local force raised by the RAF who had been made responsible for the security of Aden under the Trenchard Scheme in 1928 – were killed in an ambush by local tribesmen, that the British administration took the threat to the internal security of Aden and the Protectorate seriously. In response to an appeal by the Aden Government, British troops arrived in Aden in early July 1955.

Britain's position in the Middle East had never been quite the same since the political debacle in Palestine. The Suez campaign in 1956 hardly improved matters in the eyes of the Arabs. So Britain became the scapegoat of Arab nationalism. Abdul Nasser of Egypt, supported by Russia, spearheaded the campaign against the British presence in Aden. The brief and very successful campaign by a handful of British troops during 1955-57 in the Western Aden Protectorate against Yemen incursions and tribal lawlessness provided Nasser with evidence of 'colonial oppression'. Thus he was able to exploit the mistrust between the urban population of Aden and the less sophisticated tribesmen of the Protectorate. Nor did the 80,000 Yemenis working in Aden need much encouragement to make life as difficult as possible for the British.

The British had planned since the early 1950s to form a Federation of some or all of the states of the two Protectorates as a step towards the eventual independence of South Arabia.

Ten of the twenty States of the Western and Eastern Protectorates joined what was later to be called the Federation of South Arabia between February 1959 and February 1960. The remaining states all joined the Federation in the years up to and including 1965 – all that is except the Sultanate of Upper Yafa, which belonged to the Western Aden Protectorate, and the three Sultanates of the Eastern Protectorate, which resolutely refused to join right up to the end of the British presence in Aden. Both the Imam of the Yemen and Nasser were of course passionately opposed to the formation of the Federation. Their opposition took on a new meaning in September 1962 when, after the death of Imam Ahmed and the overthrow of his son Badr a week later by the Egyptian-backed General Sallal, a republic was declared in the Yemen. Egyptian troops were soon in evidence in the Yemen fighting against the remnants of the royalist regime. The new President scarcely attempted to disguise his opposition to the Federation. In a speech on 9th November to Yemen National Guardsmen he declared, 'I call on our brothers in the occupied South to be ready for a revolution and for joining the battle we shall wage against colonialism ...' It was hardly surprising that the House of Commons voted four days later not to recognize the Republican regime in the Yemen and to firmly support the Federation. Despite the opposition of the Yemeni-backed People's Socialist Party (PSP), Aden colony joined the Federation on 18th January 1963. A marriage between the traditionalist tribal states of the former Western Aden Protectorate and the more sophisticated and certainly wealthier former Aden Colony was bound to be difficult. But an already difficult situation was made even more so by the existence of the various other parties in this extremely complex situation – the colonial power, Britain; the Yemeni and Egyptian-backed nationalists and the Eastern Aden Protectorate states who refused to join the Federation.

Such was the situation that had evolved. Throughout 1963 relations with the Yemen deteriorated steadily. In June of that year the National Liberation Front was formed in the Yemen to carry the revolutionary struggle into Aden. It was only a matter of time before serious violence erupted. And of course it did on the morning of the 10th December when George Henderson and the innocent Indian woman bystander were killed by a grenade at Aden Airport.

The frontier with the Yemen was closed and the Federal Government declared a State of Emergency throughout South Arabia. It was now clear that an insurgency campaign was being waged against the Federation. The campaign of subversion was prosecuted mainly among the tribes of the hinterland, in particular the tribesmen of the Radfan who were offered arms, cash and promises by Yemeni and Egyptian agents to close the main road from Aden to the Yemeni frontier town of Dhala. This they were more than glad to do since the British curb in 1961 on the traditional habit of collecting 'tolls' from travellers and merchants on the Dhala road had caused great resentment and bitterness among the tribes of the Radfan. Suspicious of authority, happy to work for the highest bidder and natural warriors, the 'Red Wolves of the Radfan' made excellent guerillas. They had been brought up to regard possession of a rifle as a sign of manhood. Consequently they were excellent shots, expert judges of distance and masters of camouflage and concealment. Various estimates of the numbers of tribesmen in revolt in the Radfan have been made: the most reliable suggest that they totalled some 40,000 in all from which they were able to raise about 7,500 fighting men. They inhabited a land of mountains and defiles lying to the east of the Dhala road much of which had never been visited by a white man. The Colonial Office had only taken over official responsibility for the area in 1937 and even in 1963 were not able to enforce law and order in any permanent sense in the area. Such was the place that the British Government, after the assassination attempt on Sir Kennedy, decided to occupy.

Since the comparatively minor internal security problems of 1955, the army in Aden had lived a peaceful existence. For strategic reasons, Aden had become the site of the new HQ Middle Eastern Command in March 1961 bringing the Persian Gulf and East Africa under its operational command. The need to deploy troops in Kuwait in July 1961 justified this decision sooner than was expected. Apart from the British battalions in Aden, the Federal Regular Army (FRA), formerly the Aden Protectorate Levies, provided the bulk of the ground troops available for operations within the Federation. It was

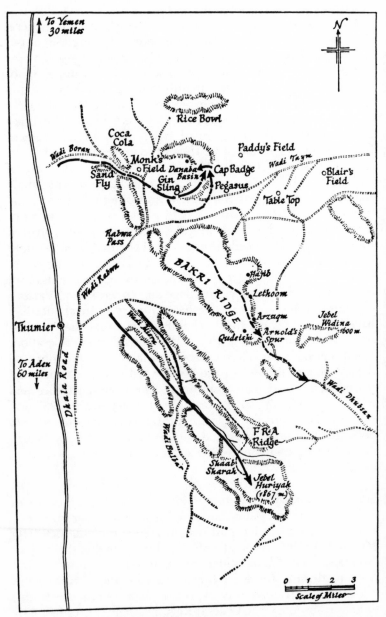

15   The capture of the Radfan in April/May 1964. The arrows indicate the main routes taken by the FRA and British forces to subdue the region

the FRA that was chosen to go into the Radfan in January 1964. Their 2nd, 3rd and 4th Battalions were supported by a troop of Centurion tanks manned by the 16th/5th Queen's Royal Lancers, a battery of 105-mm pack howitzers of the 3rd Royal Horse Artillery and a troop of Royal Engineers. Air support was no problem. Fortunately the RAF at this time were at their maximum strength in Aden. Under the command of Air Vice-Marshal J.E. Johnson, CBE, DSO, DFC at Khormaksar air base were three squadrons of Hunter GA 9 fighter ground-attack aircraft, a flight of Hunter FR 10 reconnaissance aircraft, a squadron of Belvedere HC 1 twin-rotor helicopters, four Shackleton MR 2 aircraft, as well as squadrons of Twin Pioneer, Beverley, Argosy and Valetta transport aircraft. Including a flight of three Sycamore helicopters there were in all at Khormaksar eighty-four aircraft. This was a formidable array of aircraft, many of which were made available for the Radfan operation. In addition the Royal Navy provided six Wessex helicopters.

The operation to subdue the Radfan was codenamed 'Nutcracker' and began on 4th January 1964. It was commanded by Brigadier J.D. Lunt who was commanding the FRA in Aden at the time. The operation was a demonstration of force to convince the Radfan tribesmen that the Government had the ability to enter the Radfan as and when it wished. There were two subsidiary aims, the first to put on a show of force in the Wadi Misra which was the main stronghold of the Quteibi tribe and the second to open the goat track through the Wadi Rabwa to wheeled transport so that the Wadi Taym would be accessible to military forces in the future. Using two Belvedere helicopters to place piquets on both flanks of the Wadi Rabwa and also the high ground dominating the entrance to the Wadi Misra, the FRA battalions were not only entirely successful in occupying the Wadis Rabwa and Misra but they also advanced up the Bakri Ridge and by the end of January as far north as the Wadi Taym. However the FRA simply did not have sufficient soldiers to maintain a presence on the ground that they had captured. The lack of a long-term aim proved fatal. The moment the FRA withdrew the dissidents immediately reoccupied the Radfan. This was bad for the morale of the Arab troops and of course was regarded as a victory by the tribesmen. Support from the Yemen increased even to the extent of Yemeni helicopters and MIGs attacking frontier villages and forts. The RAF retaliated by totally destroying the Yemeni frontier fort at Harib just across the border in a bomb-and-rocket-attack sortie flown by eight Hunters.

Despite 'Nutcracker', attacks on the Dhala road intensified. It was decided that a further operation would be necessary to crush the insurgency – this time involving British troops. The aim of the operation was 'to bring sufficient pressure to bear on the Radfan tribes:

    a. to prevent the tribal revolt spreading

    b. to reassert our authority

    c. to put a stop to attacks on the Dhala Road and Thumier'.

Still there was no mention of the words 'occupy' or 'secure'.

The only organized formation in Middle East Command, 24 Brigade, was at the time in Kenya. It was therefore decided to form an *ad hoc* force from Aden Garrison. This was commanded by Brigadier Louis Hargroves and on 26th April consisted of: Joint Force Headquarters, 45 Royal Marine Commando, 1st Battalion the East Anglian Regiment, B Company 3rd Battalion the Parachute Regiment (from Bahrain), A Squadron SAS, J Battery Royal Horse Artillery (RHA), A Squadron 4th Royal Tank Regiment (RTR), and two weak FRA battalions. In support there were two squadrons of Hunters, a small squadron of Shackletons, four – later six – Belvederes, a Twin Pioneer Squadron and some Scout helicopters and Beaver aircraft of 653 Squadron Army Air Corps. The first step was to establish the force at Thumier. Hargroves' first thoughts were of vertical envelopment by helicopter but, because he was lacking in up-to-date intelligence, he decided that the helicopter force was too small, valuable and vulnerable to be used in this manner. He therefore decided to capture two enormous features north of the Bakri Ridge from which he hoped to cut off the dissidents from the fertile areas thus denying them food and water and to cut their camel train routes to the Yemen. These features were nicknamed 'Cap Badge' and 'Rice Bowl'.

On 29th April the operation began when 3 Troop of A Squadron 22 SAS commanded by Captain Robin Edwards, originally of the Somerset and Cornwall Light Infantry, set out by helicopter to a Landing Zone (LZ) near to where they were due the following night to mark a Dropping Zone (DZ) for a parachute drop by 3 Para on Cap Badge. The ten men were deposited by Scout helicopters in rebel-held territory under cover of artillery fire at last light. They immediately started a night march towards the DZ. They travelled all night but by dawn were about 5,000 yards short of their objective. They decided to lie up until last light in a sangar (a circular wall of stones designed to provide cover from both view and fire).

Meanwhile at 0815 hours on the morning of the 30th April a combined force of East Anglians and 4 RTR armoured cars supported by artillery and Hunters mounted a diversionary attack up the Wadi Rabwa. The dissidents contested this advance fiercely and six soldiers were wounded by sniper fire before the guns were established at 1430 hours in a position to give covering fire on to Cap Badge.

While this action was in progress a calamity befell the SAS lying up in their sangar. A wandering goat herd had unfortunately stumbled on them during the course of the morning and before they could do anything about it they found themselves surrounded by and under fire from some forty to fifty dissidents. The patrol called for air support which was immediately provided by Hunters of 43 and 208 Squadrons. Air cover was provided throughout the entire day with aircraft diving again and again opening fire on enemy sometimes only thirty yards from the SAS patrol. Eighteen sorties were flown using 127 rockets and 7,131 rounds of ammunition. The SAS men calculated that they and the Hunters killed twenty to thirty of the enemy during the day. As night fell, however, and the Hunters could no longer provide support, a determined attack by about ninety dissidents was mounted on the ten SAS men. Trooper Warburton, the radio operator, was hit and died instantly. Captain Edwards decided that their only chance of survival lay in breaking out. This they did, firing as they ran; after only a few yards Robin Edwards was hit in the stomach by a burst of automatic fire. As he lay dying he ordered Sergeant Reg Lingham to command the break-out leaving him behind. They tried to help him but he died a few moments later. There was nothing they could do but leave him. As they charged through the dissidents they killed many of them, though three persistent rebels followed them. Coolly they waited in ambush for them, killing one and putting the others to flight. The patrol reached Thumier just after daybreak on 1st May. This incident received much publicity

when the GOC Land Forces Middle East, Major-General John
Cubbon, announced at a press conference on 3rd May that he
had reliable information of the decapitation of Edwards and
Warburton and the exhibition of their heads on stakes in Taiz.
The accusation was immediately denied by the Yemeni
Government. The GOC was castigated in the House of
Commons for making the affair public on the basis of scanty
evidence and without the approval of the Minister of Defence.
Then on 13th May a patrol of the FRA found two headless
bodies in a shallow grave in the area where the men died. The
bodies were later identified as those of Captain Edwards and
Trooper Warburton. The GOC was completely vindicated.
Thus ended the tragic but heroic affair of the SAS battle in the
mountains of the Radfan.

Another attempt the previous afternoon to insert a second
SAS party to mark the Para DZ had also failed when both Scout
helicopters were hit several times with rifle fire. Although the
Paras were willing to jump onto an unmarked and undefended
DZ, Hargroves reluctantly abandoned his plan for a Para drop
and B Company 3 Para were rushed by lorry from Khormaksar
to Thumier. Meanwhile at last light on 30th April two
companies of 45 Commando set out to occupy Rice Bowl.
Whilst on the move they were ordered by Hargroves to
consolidate on Coca Cola and Sandfly as he considered their
position on Rice Bowl untenable without the support of 3 Para
on Cap Badge. By dawn on 1st May the Commandos were firm
on these two features. There was now a lull while the
remainder of the East Anglians, who had remained in Aden
awaiting relief by the King's Own Scottish Borderers, were
brought up to Thumier.

Hargroves' plan was now that the East Anglians should
relieve 45 Commando on Coca Cola and Sandfly, while the
Commandos with B Company 3 Para under Command would
capture Cap Badge. The two companies of 45 Commando
reached the summit of Cap Badge after a brilliant night move
along the ridge leading to the feature from the south-west. The
plan was for B Company 3 Para to approach Cap Badge via the
low ground to the south of the mountain and meet up with the
Commandos on Cap Badge. Unfortunately they were caught at
first light on the morning of the 4th May on the lower slopes of
Cap Badge and in the open just below a small village from

which fairly heavy fire was opened on them by the rebels. During that day the Paras lost two killed and ten wounded. Despite heavy enemy fire they managed to eject the enemy from the village inflicting many casualties in the process. However they were overlooked by snipers in the rocks above them and were not able to break out without serious risk of further casualties to themselves. Unfortunately they were in dead ground to the Commandos on Cap Badge above them who were not able to provide supporting fire. RAF Hunters however provided close support to within 150 yards of the Para position throughout the day. So close was this support that one soldier was hit on the head and slightly injured by a 20-mm spent cannon case from one of the Hunters. Beavers of 653 Squadron Army Air Corps also flew daring resupply sorties dropping ammunition and water right into the Para position, one Beaver receiving several hits from rifle fire.

In order to extricate the Paras with the minimum of casualties the Force Commander decided at 1200 hours to move the reserve Commando company on to the top of Cap Badge by helicopter so that they could move down from above on to the rebel position dominating the Paras, the other two Commando companies remaining on Cap Badge to secure it. The move was entirely successful and the dissidents melted away. The Paras reached the top of Cap Badge that night after thirty gruelling hours in action.

Thus by the evening of 5th May Brigadier Hargroves had achieved his aim for the loss of two killed and ten wounded. During the ensuing days operations in the fertile areas continued; the Rabwa Pass was occupied and the East Anglians were introduced into the Wadi Taym. In order to maintain this pace of operations it was decided that more troops would be required. Battalion Headquarters of 3 Para were therefore moved from Bahrain to join the force and the King's Own Scottish Borderers arrived from the United Kingdom. Together with a second squadron of armoured cars provided by 4 RTR from Aden and a promise of a section of 5.5-inch guns from Singapore, this made for a sizeable reinforcement for Brigadier 'Monkey' Blacker Commanding 39 Brigade who, it was decided, should be flown from the UK with his headquarters to command phase 2 of the operations in the Radfan. Blacker's arrival allowed Hargroves and his very

successful *ad hoc* HQ to return to their proper task of internal
security in Aden. Phase 2 was planned for 26th May when
Wessex helicopters from HMS *Centaur* would be able to join
the force. In the meantime a period of intensive patrolling got
underway while the RAF operated against tribesmen on the
southern end of the Bakri Ridge as well as further to the east.

On 18th May using one company as armed porters, Colonel
Tony Farrar-Hockley* who was then commanding 3 Para,
made a rapid advance up on to the Bakri Ridge and south-east
along it down the Al Dahira Ridge, later renamed Arnold's
Spur in recognition of the incident on 20th May when
Company Sergeant-Major Arnold leading the anti-tank
platoon flushed twelve guerillas from the fortified village of Ar-
zuqm capturing three of them. By 24th May, after several
skirmishes, the Paras were in firm control of the length of the
Bakri Ridge. It was a fine example of initiative and
administrative resourcefulness. In addition to normal personal
weapons, equipment and ammunition each paratrooper
carried an average individual load of 90 lb over a distance of
some 25,000 yards. The Paras' bold action advanced the course
of the Radfan operation by at least a week.

Brigadier Blacker decided that he could now invade the most
inaccessible and cherished areas of the dissident tribesmen, the
Wadi Dhubsan and Jebel Huriyah. On 26th May the Wadi
Dhubsan was taken by 45 Commando, some men having to
descend part of the way into the wadi floor on ropes. Half-way
along the wadi the leading company encountered a sizeable
force of some thirty to fifty enemy armed with automatic
weapons as well as rifles situated in a good position on high
ground. Something of a set battle took place in which the
tribesmen fought stubbornly against 45 Commando and A
Company 3 Para who had been called up in a successful
attempt to outflank the enemy. The tribesmen continued to
pour down withering fire on the British soldiers, killing two
and wounding four Commandos, even when strafed by
Hunters and shelled by artillery and 3 Para's 3-inch mortars.
However around 1400 hours that day the tribesmen withdrew
and the Commandos and Paras gained their objective. On the
27th May the Paras were withdrawn to Thumier and thence to

---

* Now Lt-General Sir Anthony Farrar-Hockley KCB, DSO, MBE, MC

Aden. On 28th May 2 FRA relieved the Commandos on the Bakri Ridge.

The third and final phase of Blacker's operation started on 30th May. The aim was to capture the Jebel Huriyah, the highest peak in the Radfan. It was almost certain that the rebels would defend this feature as its possession was known to be a matter of prestige to them. The task of taking the Jebel Huriyah was given to the 1st East Anglians commanded by Lt-Colonel Jack Dye. They were supported by 2 FRA and D Squadron 4 RTR. The aim was to advance up the Wadi Dhubsan by means of picketing either side. This was a slow business but was achieved without any major mishap until, on 7th June, 2 FRA ran into heavy fire from a ridge (thereafter known as 'FRA Ridge') just short of and to the north of the towering Jebel Huriyah. All that day the fifty rebels on 'FRA Ridge' stood and fought despite a pounding from Hunters, J Battery of 3 RHA (105mm) and 170 (Imjin) Battery of 7 RHA (5.5in). That night, however, they melted away. The battle of 'FRA Ridge' was the turning point: foolishly the rebels had stood and fought, a fatal mistake for a guerilla force. They died or fled and did not seriously mount operations again until the end of the year. On 8th June the East Anglians established themselves on the peak of the Jebel Huriyah and saw the lights of Aden fifty miles away.

The Jebel was handed back to the RAF who reimposed the traditional methods of 'air control'. Occasionally troops were deployed to re-exert control on the ground but the emphasis was changing in South Arabia. By the end of 1964 two servicemen had been killed in Aden and thirty-four wounded in the new urban terrorist offensive launched by the National Liberation Front. The Radfan was soon to be made to look almost like a picnic in contrast to the sickening violence of Aden.

2. Aden

If a particular incident is needed to mark the beginning of the
second phase of the war in Southern Arabia it happened on the
evening of the 23rd December 1964 when a grenade was tossed
through the window of an RAF officers' quarter where a
teenage party was taking place killing the sixteen-year-old
daughter of an Air Commodore and wounding several other
children. The second and much more serious phase of the
Egyptian-inspired campaign to oust the British from Aden and
destroy the embryo Federal Government had started as it
meant to go on. There had in fact been thirty-six terrorist
incidents during 1964 in Aden but they jumped to 286 in 1965,
510 in 1966 and nearly 3,000 in the ten months before the
British departed in 1967.

The terrorist campaign had been given added impetus by the
announcement in the British Government Defence White
Paper of July 1964 that South Arabia would be granted its
independence not later than 1968. However, although
independence was planned, military independence was not.
The intention at this juncture was to maintain a British military
base in Aden. Now that the date for independence was set, the
Egyptians and the various national movements they supported
set about gaining power for themselves by 1968. There were
three main nationalist groups; they were the South Arabian
League (SAL), the National Liberation Front (NLF) and the
Front for the Liberation of Occupied South Yemen (FLOSY).
The most formidable of these from the military point of view
was the NLF because it was they who, from the start, firmly
espoused violence as the best and most effective means of
achieving their aims. The NLF was solely responsible for all
acts of terrorism in Aden State until early 1966 and for most of
them after that. Both SAL and FLOSY, however, believed in
political action to achieve their aims though FLOSY resorted
to violence, not only against the British but also against the
NLF, in 1966-7. The aim of FLOSY was the union of both the
Federation and Aden State with the Yemen. These then were
the organizations which the British Army was to face and they

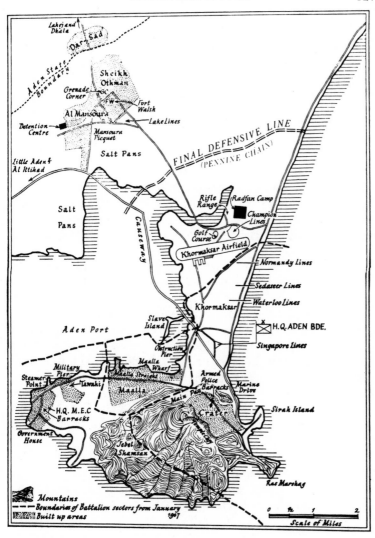

16   Aden town: showing the battalion sectors of responsibility

followed the traditional techniques and tactics of intimidation, industrial action and propaganda that terrorists before them had employed against the British elsewhere in the Middle East in Palestine and Cyprus.

The geography of Aden State needs explanation in order to understand the complex events of 1965–67. In the north nearest to the land frontier with the Yemen and astride the frontier with Lahej lay the twin towns of Dar Saad and Sheikh Othman both of which were used by the terrorists as 'mounting areas' for many of their operations in Crater. Sheikh Othman in particular was regarded by the Security Forces as perhaps the most troublesome Arab township in Aden State. To the west of and adjacent to Sheikh Othman was Al Mansoura which contained the detention centre where those suspected of terrorist activities were detained under the Emergency Powers Act.

Further west and *en route* to Little Aden was the newly constructed federal capital of Al Ittihad which, along with the BP oil refinery and the 24 Infantry Brigade military cantonment in Little Aden, presented an enormous security problem. All these installations had to be constantly guarded.

Across the isthmus, on which lay Khormaksar Airfield and Radfan Camp, was the town of Aden, itself divided into its four constituent parts: Steamer Point, Tawahi, Maalla and Crater. The latter which was predominantly an Arab town was regarded by Arabs as the true capital of Aden State. Steamer Point contained Government House and Headquarters Middle East Command (HQ MEC); Tawahi was the main business and shopping centre and Maalla, as well as being an Arab township, contained many service married quarters.

In January 1965 Sir Richard Turnbull succeeded Sir Kennedy Trevaskis as High Commissioner to the Federation of South Arabia. He was in overall charge of defence and internal security matters advised as necessary by the Commander in Chief Middle East, who delegated effective control of internal security to the GOC Land Forces, who had at his disposal the Aden Brigade, the HQ of which was at Singapore Lines on the isthmus, and 24 Brigade with its HQ in Little Aden.

In early March one Abdul Mackawee, previously leader of the Opposition People's Socialist Party, was appointed Chief Minister of the Aden State Government. An ardent nationalist, Mackawee ensured that every security measure promulgated by the High Commissioner was opposed and criticized and that every accusation against British troops was upheld and encouraged. On 22nd April he dissociated himself and his Government from the curfew imposed by the High Commissioner following an attack on the Aden Commissioner of Prisons. By now it was apparent that more troops would be needed and in late April the total garrison was raised to five battalions by the despatch of the 1st Royal Sussex from Malta.

On 5th June the new GOC Land Forces, Major-General John Willoughby, was also appointed Security Commander, a new post designed to encourage greater co-operation not only between the two brigades in Aden but also between government, the police, the intelligence community and the other service chiefs. The following day the High Commissioner introduced Emergency Regulations in Aden State which enabled him to detain suspects without trial for up to six months and to proscribe any terrorist organizations which he believed were engaged in subversion or terrorism.

On 29th August Arthur Barrie, a senior British police officer, was shot dead in Crater. Then, ten days later, Sir Arthur Charles, the British Speaker of the Aden State Legislative Council, was ambushed and killed by a gunman – also in Crater. Thus terrorism continued at sporadic intervals in Aden.

The momentum was still maintained, however, in the Radfan. The Royal Engineers carried out an extensive programme of road building, particularly in the Rabwa Pass. The 2nd Battalion the Coldstream Guards unfortunately lost three men killed near the Dhala road in March and the following month 50 Field Squadron Royal Engineers suffered two killed and five wounded during a furious attack by tribesmen on their base camp. Casualties were by no means one-sided, however: the 1st Royal Sussex killed four tribesmen and wounded some more in a successful ambush during July. But it was in Aden that the real battle was being fought. On 17th September a grenade was thrown among a party of British schoolchildren at Khormaksar Airport who were waiting to fly back to the United Kingdom after their summer holidays. Five children were injured, two of them seriously. As a result of this incident and the others which preceded it the High Commissioner dissolved the Aden Government and assumed direct rule. In the ensuing riot the 1st Prince of Wales Own

Regiment of Yorkshire and the FRA between them arrested some 750 rioting Arabs, many of whom were deported to the Yemen.

In all military operations in Aden, the British Army was bound, as it has been in many other counter-insurgency situations, by the principle of 'minimum force'. By and large troops could only shoot if they had already been shot at. The decision as to what degree of force to use in a particular situation was left to the senior man on the spot which, in the case of a lone sentry, was himself. Written instructions were issued to all ranks – in much the same way as they were later to be issued in Northern Ireland. Provided an individual acted in 'good faith', the Security Commander made it absolutely clear that he accepted full responsibility for the actions of all the soldiers under his command. With very few exceptions it is true to say that the rule of minimum force was strictly adhered to; indeed there were instances when British soldiers lost their lives when they hesitated to open fire for fear of shooting the wrong man. The principle of 'minimum force' is consistent with the British way of doing things and though, in a purely military context, it may not be the simplest and quickest way of solving a military problem, British troops in Aden showed a remarkable awareness of the political consequences of the irresponsible use of military force. It is probably true to say that no other army has so consistently abided by this principle in the face of such extreme provocation.

By the end of 1965 six British soldiers had been killed and eighty-three wounded. The largest proportion of these casualties were caused by grenades. In the narrow streets of Aden every door and window presented an opportunity for the terrorist, who could throw or drop his grenade and then slip round the corner and sit nonchalantly in a coffee house with not a shred of evidence to indicate his guilt. Rocket launchers were also used by the terrorists during 1965, though by the beginning of 1966 these gave way to mortars which had greater range and flexibility. If 1965 had been a bad year, 1966 was to be even worse. Though the number of British soldiers killed during 1966 was only five, the total wounded jumped to 218. This was perhaps surprising because on the 22nd February the new British Government announced that after all, a British military presence would not be maintained in Aden after independence. There was now in theory little to be achieved from killing British soldiers since they were going to go anyway. But logic does not always prevail.

The decision of the 22nd February was in line with the new Labour Administration's policy of withdrawal from all remaining military commitments East of Suez as quickly as possible. The Federal rulers were of course shattered by what they understandably regarded as British perfidy. It had been largely the assurance of British military backing that had persuaded them to agree to federation in the first place. On the other hand President Nasser and the nationalist movements he supported in Aden were much encouraged. From the point of view of the army the announcement was a disastrous one. What little local support they had enjoyed would now be totally removed. The army was once again put in the firing line.

In January the Aden Brigade was enlarged to four battalions with the arrival of the 1st Battalion the South Wales Borderers. Their arrival coincided with a steady increase in violence which culminated in the showdown of the 11th–14th February. Both major terrorist organizations planned a day of violence on the 11th February which was the eighth anniversary of the formation of the federation. They dramatically christened this day, the aim of which was to demonstrate that the British could not keep the peace in Aden, 'The Day of the Volcano'. By deploying the Aden Brigade, now consisting of the 3rd Royal Anglians, 1st Royal Northumberland Fusiliers, the 1st South Wales Borderers and the 1st Cameronians supported by one squadron of armoured cars supplied by the Queen's Dragoon Guards (QDG), on 10th February terrorist plans were pre-empted. Although there were some incidents, the massive violence planned never got off the ground. On 30th April a terrorist bomb in Sheikh Othman demolished a school bus killing nine children and injuring another fourteen. It was at this stage that the evacuation of British service families was started and a new Security Commander, General Philip Tower, was appointed. At the same time Sir Richard Turnbull was succeeded as High Commissioner by Sir Humphrey Trevelyan who had been appointed to oversee the British withdrawal from Aden. The stage was now set for the final act of this sordid drama for which the authorities had thoughtfully provided a new cast.

On 24th May the 3rd Royal Anglians handed over Radfan

Camp to the 1st Battalion the Parachute Regiment commanded by Lt-Colonel Michael Walsh*. In their area of responsibility lay Sheikh Othman where law and order had virtually completely broken down. All manner of arms including rockets and mortars were in regular use by the terrorists. Within a week of arrival it was decided to deploy the Paras in Sheikh Othman in anticipation of a general strike which had been announced for the 1st June. In the early hours of that day the Paras occupied the Police Station in Sheikh Othman as well as seven other roof-top observation posts.

As soon as the terrorists discovered the Paras were in their midst an unholy battle between the Paras and NLF snipers and grenadiers broke out and lasted for twenty-four hours. One Para was killed and four wounded during what became later known amongst Paras as 'The Glorious First of June' but six terrorist kills were confirmed and five more were captured. The Paras remained in Sheikh Othman until they handed over to the South Arabian Army (SAA), formerly the FRA, in September. Tragically, though, there were to be major complications in relations with the SAA before September. The first rumblings were on 16th June when a group of senior Arab officers objected to the appointment of a new commander designate of the SAA. Because they did not put their complaint through the proper channels they were suspended from duty pending an investigation. On the morning of 20th June rumour had it that these officers had been arrested and dismissed by the British authorities; troops rioted, seized armouries and put their barracks in a state of defence to repel the attack which it was rumoured the British were mounting against the SAA. The first casualties were nineteen men of the Royal Corps of Transport who were driving innocently past Champion Lines returning from a rifle range practice. They were ambushed at close range by a hail of fire from the barrack huts of the Arab soldiers. Eight British soldiers were killed and another eight wounded. In the ensuing crossfire two policemen, a British Public Works employee and a subaltern of the Lancashire Fusiliers on duty in the nearby Radfan Camp were also killed.

C Company of the 1st Battalion the King's Own Border Regiment was ordered to restore the situation in Champion

---

* Now Major-General M.J.H. Walsh, DSO.

Lines – if possible without firing a round! Supported by a troop of armoured cars of the Queen's Dragoon Guards they set out for Champion Lines. Coming a little too close, they were shot at as they dismounted from their vehicles losing one killed and eight wounded. A platoon of the Borderers immediately made a dash for the SAA Guardroom without themselves opening fire, although they were given some covering fire by the armoured cars. Two other platoons then occupied the rest of the camp. As the SAA soldiers saw that the British were not firing at them all opposition melted away. A highly complex situation had been solved in a way which perhaps only the British Army would attempt. Major David Miller, the Borderer company officer in command of the operation, was awarded the Military Cross and two of his company Mentioned in Dispatches.

But the horror of the 20th June was not over. The rumours of an attack by the British had spread to the Police Barracks in Crater. Major John Moncur commanding Y Company of the 1st Battalion the Royal Northumberland Fusiliers (RNF) had just at that time lost contact with one of his platoons which he had ordered to withdraw from a position near the Police Barracks in Crater. Worried about them, he decided to go and look for them himself. He and his party were mounted in two landrovers and he was accompanied by his company sergeant-major, four men of his own company, and Major Brian Malcolm and two soldiers from the Argyll and Sutherland Highlanders who were due to take over responsibility for Crater shortly. As the group approached the Police Barracks they came under heavy fire at almost point-blank range. All except one man were killed. At about the same time, just after midday, another party of British soldiers narrowly escaped death. The pilot of an army Sioux helicopter was hit in the knee by a bullet just as he was landing a two-man RNF piquet into position on the rim of the volcano overlooking Crater. One of the passengers was knocked unconscious and badly injured in the forced landing but the other, Fusilier Duffy, pulled both the pilot and his brother fusilier clear of the blazing helicopter before it exploded, radioed for help, tended his comrades' wounds and guarded them until help arrived. For his bravery Fusilier Duffy was awarded the Distinguished Conduct Medal.

During the afternoon two attempts were made to re-enter

Crater. Both were driven off by intense small arms and rocket fire. It would have been perfectly possible to retake Crater at this stage in a full-scale operation using the 76-mm guns of the Saladin Armoured Cars and accepting the risk of a high casualty rate. But the price would almost certainly have been the complete alienation of the SAA and the Aden Police, which were likely to be the only indigenous organizations capable of running the federation after independence, and heavy casualties among the civil population. So General Tower was forced to take the militarily unpopular but politically necessary decision not to retake Crater that day.

The 20th June 1967 was a tragic and terrible day for the army in Aden. In all twenty-two soldiers were killed and thirty-one wounded. The extent of the casualties was no reflection on their professionalism for they had been mown down, not in combat, but by men who they thought were their comrades. The dead were buried five days later twenty-five miles from Crater in a blasted stretch of desert called Silent Valley.

Meanwhile Crater was ringed by troops. British snipers methodically picked off anyone seen carrying a weapon illegally and succeeded in killing ten terrorists in this way. The policy of at all cost avoiding civilian bloodshed in Crater dictated that the area would have to be taken by stealth. SAS patrols slipped into Crater at night and confirmed that the Arabs were almost without exception off their guard through most of the night. Lt-Colonel Colin Mitchell, commanding the Argyll and Sutherland Highlanders who had just assumed responsibility for Crater from the RNF, was ordered to re-enter Crater on the night of 3rd July. Although General Tower had intended that it should be a limited 'nibbling' operation, Colonel Mitchell was given permission at the very last moment by Brigadier Charles Dunbar acting on behalf of General Tower to push ahead as far as the Chartered Bank building which was the tallest building in the commercial centre of Crater. In the event he went even beyond this. What is more he took some newspaper reporters with him. Next morning the Argylls were in firm control of most of Crater having suffered no casualties themselves and having killed two terrorist gunmen. Their achievement is all the more remarkable in that they had never set foot in Crater before having only just arrived from England. The whole battalion had, however, firmly imprinted every alleyway and building in Crater in their mind's eye on scale models painstakingly built in their barracks back in England.

After dark on 4th July the remainder of Crater, including the Armed Police Barracks, was occupied. Colonel Mitchell continued to say exactly what he thought and do more or less exactly what he pleased and put up the backs of virtually every senior officer in Aden, particularly Philip Tower, in the process. Mitchell was an unconventional man to say the least. He certainly captured the imagination of the British people back at home for whom he became an instant hero. Whatever the merits and demerits of his style he kept a firm hand on Crater for the remainder of the British occupation.

On 13th July the Armed Police in Crater paraded for and were inspected by General Tower. These were the men who had killed British soldiers on 20th June. At about the same time 20th November was announced as the planning date for final withdrawal. It was now a matter of hanging on. August was a terrible month in which there were over 700 terrorist incidents causing twenty casualties among British troops. Little Aden was handed over to the SAA on 13th September by the Queen's Own Hussars (QOH) and later the same month 1 Para left the SAA in charge of the furious battle now raging between the NLF and FLOSY in Sheikh Othman. (The NLF had already gained control of the former Aden Protectorate soon after the last British troops had withdrawn to Aden at the end of June. By the 31st August all but one of the States of the Federation were under their control and the Federal Government had effectively ceased to exist.) When 1 Para withdrew from Sheikh Othman they had spent four months there, during which time they had had three men killed and twenty-one wounded. During the same period they killed thirty-two terrorists and wounded thirteen. From Sheikh Othman they withdrew to a prepared defensive line which stretched across the isthmus about two miles north of Khormaksar Airfield. This line known as the Pennine Chain had been prepared by 1 Para and 3 Troop 60 Field Squadron Royal Engineers during the previous week. It was held by 1 Para, who had under their command C Squadron of the QOH and 31 Battery of 45 Light Regiment Royal Artillery, until the day before the final withdrawal from Aden.

September and October were comparatively quiet months

for the Security Forces as the NLF and FLOSY slogged it out. During this period the South Wales Borderers and the Lancashire Regiment returned to England. Both regiments had distinguished themselves, but particularly the Lancashires who won six decorations in action including a DSO for their commanding officer. On 11th October 42 Royal Marine Commando arrived in Aden aboard the commando carrier HMS *Albion*. Their role was to act as rearguard for the final British withdrawal, a role for which they were particularly suited having HMS *Albion* as their offshore base for operations and the ship's helicopters to take them to and fro.

On 6th November the SAA declared their support for the NLF, and on 13th November the British Government agreed to negotiate with the NLF. By 25th November only about 3,500 servicemen remained in Aden. On 26th November three battalions of the SAA, now calling themselves the Arab Armed Forces in Occupied South Yemen, took over from 42 and 45 Commandos and the Argylls in Maalla, Tawahi, and Crater respectively. On 27th November the High Commissioner went aboard HMS *Eagle* offshore and the remaining British troops withdrew to an enclave around Khormaksar Airfield protected by 1 Para on the Pennine Chain in the north and 45 Commando positioned at the narrowest point of the isthmus in the south. The thinning-out process continued throughout the 28th and the morning of the 29th November. The final scene was played at 1450 hours on the afternoon of the 29th when the last company of 42 Commando was flown out by Wessex helicopter to their carrier, HMS *Albion*. Major-General Philip Tower was on the last but one helicopter to leave. South Arabia became independent at midnight.

The price paid by the British Army in Radfan and Aden from 1964–67 was ninety lives lost and 510 wounded. Once again the army was required to hold the ring while politicians and diplomats scurried to and fro trying to patch something up. Whether, in view of what Aden has since become, the effort and the cost in lives can be said to have been worth it is doubtful. The young soldiers in Aden faced extreme provocation and continuous danger in very unglamorous circumstances – that they did so so steadfastly and uncomplainingly is truly remarkable. It is a story of which the army can justly feel proud.

12

Northern Ireland
1969–84

Clearly any attempt to chronicle the Emergency in Ulster over the past fourteen years in one chapter can only be superficial and selective in its treatment of what is manifestly a complex, tragic and seemingly endless struggle. This chapter can only outline the main milestones of the campaign and highlight certain incidents which are hopefully illustrative of the wider picture.

Eire's relations with the United Kingdom both before and since Independence have of course always been stormy. The Irish Republican Army (IRA) emerged as the military arm of the Sinn Fein ('Ourselves Alone') movement following the 1918 elections; it employed guerilla tactics against the British Army. This turned into civil war when some Sinn Feiners refused to accept the Anglo-Irish Treaty of 6th December 1921. In the south the installations of the new Free State Government were attacked and in the north there was a bitter Protestant backlash in which 232 people were killed and 1,000 injured. There were sporadic insurrections in the thirties and in 1939 the attacks switched to England where some nasty bomb explosions occurred. Soldiers on leave in Ulster during the Second World War thought twice about walking down the Falls Road in Belfast in uniform. The campaign of 1956–62 failed to get off the ground properly because the IRA never really got the public support that they needed.

In February 1967, however, the Northern Ireland Civil Rights Association was formed. It organized a series of marches and demonstrations throughout Northern Ireland

17   Northern Ireland

during 1968 to protest against gerrymandering and plural
voting to the disadvantage of the Catholic minority and against
undoubted discrimination in matters of housing and jobs.
'One man – one vote' was adopted as the marching slogan of
the movement. Few disagree that the Catholic minority in
Ulster had been discriminated against for years. A few
examples will suffice.

The basis for the drawing up of ward boundaries is
complicated but essentially the 1854 Towns Improvement
(Ireland) Act stated that wards should be formed having regard
to 'the number of persons rated in each ward, as well as to the
aggregate amount of the sums at which all the said persons
shall be so rated'. This act was repealed but its provisions were
repeated in the Local Government (Northern Ireland) Act
1922. In practice in many cases a large proportion of poorer
property is included in one ward, so that few votes are needed
in wealthier wards to return a member. Given the tendency to
live in segregated groups and that the more valuable property
is usually Protestant, the division of an area to produce a
permanent majority for one side is not difficult. In

Londonderry, Armagh and Omagh the percentage of Catholics in the population in 1968 was 69 per cent, 59 per cent and 61 per cent respectively but the Unionists held twelve out of twenty, twelve out of twenty and twelve out of twenty-one seats in the councils respectively. In 1967 in Londonderry where Catholic voters numbered 14,429 and other voters 8,781 Unionists held twelve seats on the Council and non-Unionists eight. The examples are endless. There are equally appalling examples in both housing and jobs.

The problem of course goes very deep; Irishmen have given to the terms 'Catholic' and 'Protestant' a meaning which would not be understood anywhere else in the Christian world. The terms do not necessarily in themselves have any intrinsic religious significance. An advertisement which appeared in a Belfast newspaper illustrated this beautifully: 'Wanted: Reliable cook-general. Protestant (Christian preferred)'. In Ulster, whatever else one is, one is born a Catholic or a Protestant and this divide is encouraged and perpetuated by a segregated system of religious education.

It was for these reasons and against this background that the Civil Rights Movement gained momentum throughout 1968. On 5th October a major civil rights parade took place in Londonderry at which rioting broke out. During a similar march the following January from Belfast to Londonderry the marchers were set upon in the village of Burntollet by Protestant thugs who beat up and severely injured many marchers. As the year progressed the rioting became more serious. During the weekend of 20th–21st April over 200 members of the Royal Ulster Constabulary (RUC) and seventy-nine civilians were injured in Londonderry. Various acts of sabotage took place in country areas against water mains and electricity sub-stations. The IRA were beginning to climb on the bandwagon. The violent action of some of its members prompted a split in the organization's ranks. The nationalist wing became the Provisional Army Council and sought a direct confrontation with the traditional enemy at the end of which they hoped a Republic of thirty-two counties would emerge. The Provisional Army Council thus created the Provisional IRA usually referred to as PIRA or the 'Provisionals'. The Official IRA or 'Officials' which is a Marxist organization took a longer-term view and aimed to create without violence a

United Ireland in which the working classes of both religious persuasions would co-exist. Differences between the two wings of the IRA have frequently reached feud proportions during the Emergency in Northern Ireland.

In August 1969 there was serious rioting in Belfast. This reached a climax on the 14th when eight people were killed, 170 houses in Belfast were destroyed and the cost of damage to life and property rose to some £8 million. It was at this stage on 13th August, when the RUC had clearly lost control, that the Government took the fateful step of dispatching troop reinforcements to Ulster for deployment in the streets. Garrison troops had been used earlier in the year to guard key installations but the August decision meant that British troops had been deployed to quell riots in a British city. The soldiers were welcomed as saviours by the bulk of the Catholic population. Although the IRA was not slow to make political capital out of the genuine sense of grievance felt by the Civil Rights Movement, the violence had been hitherto almost entirely sectarian and not aimed at the army. However it was not long before PIRA gunmen started to shoot at soldiers struggling to keep Catholic and Protestant crowds apart. It was on 17th August that PIRA officially announced in Dublin that their northern units had been defending Catholic areas which had been 'attacked by deliberately fomented sectarian forces ... with the aim of destroying the natural solidarity and unity of working-class people'.

Serious rioting during which men of the 3rd Battalion the Light Infantry came under sniper fire occurred in the Shankill area of Belfast in October 1969. Fortunately on this occasion no soldiers were killed though some thirteen were wounded. There followed a brief lull until the IRA bombing campaign started in January 1970. Ominously the first Catholic riot against troops occurred on 3rd March. The welcome given to the British soldiers the previous summer by the Catholic population was beginning to turn sour. PIRA propaganda had been remarkably successful. In April troop reinforcements were sent to the Province and the GOC, General Sir Ian Freeland, announced that anyone seen carrying or throwing a petrol bomb was liable to be shot. The bombing campaign however continued throughout April and into May. In June serious rioting resulted in five civilian deaths and many injured

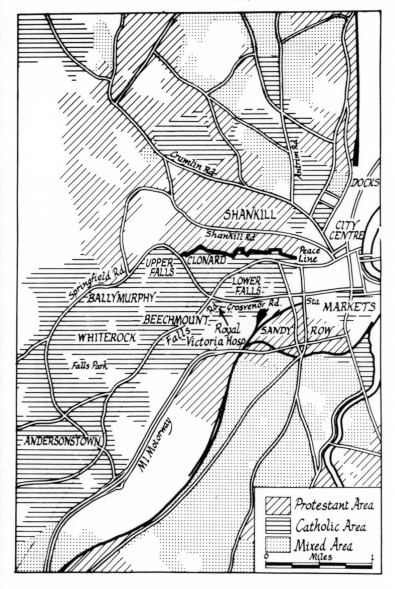

18 West Belfast; the focus of unrest in Belfast, showing the significant sectarian divisions

but this was only a foretaste of the riots in the Lower Falls area of Belfast between the 3rd and 5th July. The disturbances were sparked off after a successful search by men of the Royal Scots of a house in Balkan Street in the Lower Falls in which fifteen pistols, a rifle and a sub-machine-gun and a quantity of ammunition were found. For three days the Royal Scots, the 2nd Battalion the Queen's Regiment and the Devon and Dorset Regiment battled with rioters who hijacked city buses to form barricades across the streets and who threw nail and petrol bombs indiscriminately at them. Several gunmen engaged the troops with extremely accurate sniper fire. At the end of the three days thirteen soldiers were admitted to hospital suffering from gunshot wounds and a further five from grenade-splinter wounds. Four civilians died from gunshot wounds and well over 300 people were injured. Vast quantities of weapons, ammunition and explosives were found in houses in the Lower Falls.

It seems in retrospect that the senseless orgy of violence that the people of the Lower Falls engaged in that July made them perhaps question – if only temporarily – the course they were set on. In August a ban on all parades and marches was imposed by the Northern Ireland Government for six months. Terrorism continued in a small way but by and large people seemed to be taking stock.

The storm broke again the following February. Again it was anger resulting from a successful search for arms that brought the crowds onto the streets again. This time the violence spread all over the Province. On 8th February Lance-Bombardier Laurie of 32 Heavy Regiment Royal Artillery received gunshot wounds in the head when his landrover was ambushed in Belfast's Crumlin Road. He died a few days later. On 10th February five BBC employees were killed in County Fermanagh by a land mine that had been intended for a military patrol while on their way to check a faulty transmitter. On 11th March three young Scottish soldiers, two of whom were under the age of eighteen, were abducted from a pub, where they had been drinking, and murdered. Their bodies were found in a ditch in Ligoniel on the outskirts of Belfast. The subsequent furore in the press forced the Ministry of Defence to announce that henceforward soldiers under the age of eighteen would not be permitted to serve in the Province.

On 20th March Major James Chichester-Clark resigned as Prime Minister of Ulster. Chichester-Clark, an honest country gentleman of limited shrewdness and political acumen, had replaced the dilettante Captain Terence O'Neill in April 1969. Whereas O'Neill had unashamedly upheld the Protestant Supremacy while at the same time managing to utter soothing platitudes about equal rights for all Ulstermen, Chichester-Clark had genuinely tried to remove some of the more glaring inequalities. He had for instance approved the setting up of the Hunt Commission which recommended in October 1969 that the hated so-called 'B-Specials' (an armed Volunteer Police Reserve which had recruited exclusively from the Protestant community) should be disbanded. Chichester-Clark was replaced on 23rd March by Brian Faulkner, an able middle-class businessman of Presbyterian values who was prepared to go to almost any lengths to preserve the British connection.

Faulkner inherited a rapidly worsening situation. PIRA was now engaged in open war and it was a terrorist campaign rather than the continuing communal violence which had by the summer of 1971 become the main preoccupation of the Security Forces. From the start of 1971 the incidence of terrorism had been showing an alarming increase: by early August twelve British soldiers, two policemen and sixteen civilians had died as a result of the growing violence in the Province. Bomb explosions had long since become a daily occurrence. On 9th August a soldier was shot in the head in Belfast and died instantly. Throughout that day mobs roamed the streets burning and looting. There was now no doubt that the Provisionals had launched a full scale terrorist campaign against the civilian population of Northern Ireland. The police had lost control in many Catholic areas; witnesses, intimidated by the IRA, would not give evidence; even juries were in danger convicting. In a situation where terrorist intimidation, plus some degree of sympathy with the terrorists among a large section of the community, exists, the successful arrest and conviction of terrorist criminals becomes virtually impossible; in such circumstances some alternative must be found for the normal procedures of criminal justice. In Ireland, both North and South, this has traditionally been detention and internment without trial. In the inter-war and post-war years it had been accepted that the use of internment was necessary to public order. Neither Whitehall nor the Army were particularly keen on the idea. Reluctantly in the face of the increasing violence in August and under pressure from Faulkner, Maudling who was then Home Secretary gave his consent. The arrest operation began at 0430 hours on 9th August and predictably caused a violent reaction throughout the Province. The net was cast fairly wide and internees varied from known terrorists to comparatively harmless pamphleteers.* Early in the operation a small batch of suspected terrorists were chosen for in-depth interrogation by army experts. The same methods were regularly used by the army to train their soldiers to themselves resist interrogation. The methods were inevitably frightening and psychologically disorientating and intentionally so. But they did not involve physical force nor was any physical injury inflicted. In March 1972 the whole question of in-depth interrogation was examined by a committee under Lord Parker. The committee found that the duress to which those under interrogation had been subjected did not amount to brutality. Above all it found that the information gleaned from these methods was indispensable in the fight against the IRA. The government decided however to follow the advice of Lord Gardiner who, in a minority report, advised that the practice be discontinued. Much was written subsequently about the use of 'White Noise' and other methods of disorientation. Much later Britain was put in the dock in the European Court of Human Rights which, in the rarefied atmosphere of a courtroom, was bound to find against the practice. In reality the army had used highly sophisticated and clinical, though admittedly and intentionally very frightening methods, to get vital information from evil men. Whether their continued use would have been the vital weapon to defeat the IRA we shall never know.

On 6th October Faulkner announced that three more battalions would be deployed in Ulster bringing the troop level to 13,600. Most of these additional troops were deployed in the border areas where troops cratering border crossing points regularly came under fire from terrorist groups inside Eire. During 1971 forty-three British soldiers were killed. The newly formed Ulster Defence Regiment (UDR) composed mainly of

---

* Detention without trial was ended on 5th December 1975.

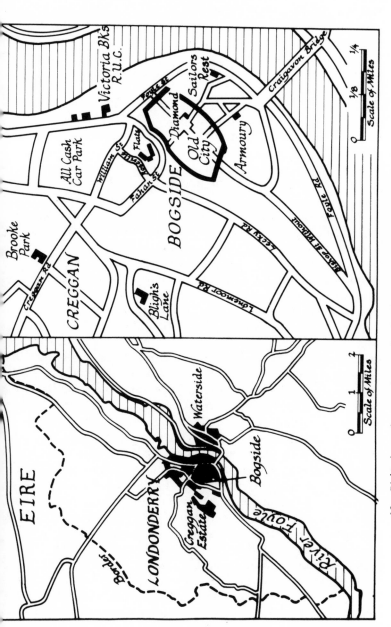

19 *Right*, the enclave on the west bank of the River Foyle which includes the old city of Londonderry, the Bogside and the Creggan, and *left*, detail of the Bogside area of the city where the events of 'Bloody Sunday', 30th January 1972, took place

part time soldiers had five men killed, the RUC another eleven. In addition sixty-one civilians died in the violence during the year. The only consolation – if it can be called that – was that fifty-two Republican terrorists were killed by the Security Forces.

On 30th January 1972 occurred in Londonderry what has since become known as 'Bloody Sunday'. A Sunday afternoon protest march was infiltrated by hooligans determined to provoke a confrontation with the troops policing the march. The Brigade Commander decided to mount an operation to attempt to arrest some of the hooligans who by 3.30 pm were hurling stones, bricks and even CS grenades at his soldiers. At 5.55 pm a shot was fired at soldiers of the 1st Battalion the Parachute Regiment (1 PARA) who were in occupation of a house in William Street. Immediately following this incident two 1 PARA soldiers shot dead a man lighting a nail bomb. Minutes later 1 PARA went into the area of the Rosseville Flats from three directions in an attempt to cut off as many of the hooligans as possible. As they dismounted from their 'Pigs' (armoured one-ton trucks) they came under fire. A burst from what was probably a Thompson sub-machine-gun struck the ground around them. It seemed to come from the Rosseville Flats. Simultaneously one or more gunmen opened up from the direction of Rosseville Street. Then several nail bombs were thrown at the Para soldiers. What looked like three armed men were seen running across the open ground in front of the flats and were engaged. It was at this stage and during the minutes that followed that thirteen civilians died of gunshot wounds. Their death attracted great publicity and 1 PARA were accused of 'sheer unadulterated murder' by the Londonderry City Coroner. The controversy has raged ever since. Perhaps the only constructive way to comment upon the affair is to quote verbatim the relevant conclusions of the Widgery Report which was published on 10th April 1972. Conclusion 1 reads: 'There would have been no deaths in Londonderry on 30th January if those who organized the illegal march had not thereby created a highly dangerous situation in which a clash between demonstrators and the Security Forces was almost inevitable.' Conclusion 3 reads: 'If the Army had persisted in its "low key" attitude and had not launched a large scale operation to arrest the hooligans the day might have passed off without serious incident.' Conclusion 7 reads: 'When the vehicles and soldiers of Support Company appeared in Rosseville Street they came under fire. Arrests were made but in a very short time the arrest operation took second place and the soldiers turned to engage their assailants. There is no reason to suppose that the soldiers would have opened fire if they had not been fired upon first.' Conclusion 8 reads: 'Soldiers who identified armed gunmen fired upon them in accordance with the standing order in the Yellow Card. Each soldier was his own judge of whether he had identified a gunman. Their training made them aggressive and quick in decision and some showed more restraint in opening fire than others. At one end of the scale some soldiers showed a high degree of responsibility; at the other, notably in Glenfada Park, firing bordered on the reckless. These distinctions reflect differences in the character and temperament of the soldiers concerned.' Finally Conclusion 11 reads: 'There was no general breakdown in discipline. For the most part the soldiers acted as they did because they thought their orders required it. No order and no training can ensure that a soldier will always act wisely, as well as bravely and with initiative. The individual soldier ought not to have to bear the burden of deciding whether to open fire in confusion such as prevailed on 30th January. In the conditions prevailing in Northern Ireland, however, this is often inescapable.'

These paragraphs really say it all. There must be an inherent danger in using troops who are trained for war and to be aggressive in a situation such as so often prevails in Ulster.

An open verdict was recorded on the victims of Bloody Sunday at the inquest in Londonderry. As a military operation the Para sortie into the Bogside was highly successful; the political consequences though were catastrophic.

The bombing campaign reached its height in 1972. There were in fact 1,853 bomb incidents among the most horrific of which were the Aldershot Officers' Mess bomb in February which killed seven people; the Abercorn Restaurant explosion in March which killed two girls and injured many more; the many bombs of 'Bloody Friday' 21st July which killed seven people in Belfast; the virtual destruction of the village of Claudy on 31st July by three enormous car bombs which killed

six people; the 500-lb bomb which exploded on 10th
September under a Saracen armoured personnel carrier on
patrol in County Tyrone which was large enough to throw the
vehicle and its occupants off the road and over a hedge killing
three soldiers. 1972 saw more violence than any other year in
the campaign. There were more bombings, more shootings,
more soldiers killed, more terrorists killed and more civilian
casualties. Many Irishmen could not believe that it had come
to this. The despair of the majority of the people was pitiful to
behold.

The army, despite the enormous pressure it was now under,
managed to keep up the pressure on the IRA. Perhaps the
greatest success of 1972 was Operation Motorman which took
place on 31st July. For months the Provisionals had controlled
the Creggan and Bogside areas of Londonderry as well as parts
of Belfast. These areas had become so-called 'No Go' areas for
the Security Forces. Intelligence indicated that an attempt to
take the 'No Go' areas, in which gunmen openly patrolled and
manned roadblocks, would result in massive civilian casualties.
The political decision was therefore taken not to interfere thus
permitting gun law to rule for a time in parts of two cities of
the United Kingdom. Finally however it was decided enough
was enough. Among the armoured vehicles that went into the
Bogside were four Royal Engineer Centurion bulldozer tanks
which quickly removed the barricades. They had been specially
brought into the Province for the operation. A parallel
operation in Belfast involving eleven battalions went off
equally smoothly. There was in fact little resistance in either
Londonderry or Belfast though two snipers were shot dead by
Security Forces. Most importantly a military presence was
re-established in the 'No Go' areas.

The incidence of terrorism in the area of the border with the
Republic increased in 1971 and 1972. By 1973 regiments
deployed in Fermanagh, Tyrone, and Armagh were having a
particularly busy time. It was in the rural areas that the
regiments of the Royal Armoured Corps came into their own.
Their Saracens, Ferrets and Saladins were proof against
small-arms fire but vulnerable to the culvert and milk churn
bombs that the IRA were now beginning to use with increasing
regularity. South Armagh usually referred to as 'bandit
country' by the press became in the years 1973–79 probably the

most dangerous area in Northern Ireland. Cross-border gun battles regularly took place and army bases such as Crossmaglen could only be supplied by helicopter. The part played by the Puma and Wessex helicopters of the RAF and the smaller Sioux, Scout, Gazelle and Lynx helicopters of the Army Air Corps has been vital. They have been used for logistic re-supply, for surveillance, for casualty evacuation and for deploying troops in to ambush or roadblock positions. They have become an indispensable tool of the Security Forces.

Whether on the border on a 'rural tour' or in Belfast or Londonderry on an 'urban tour', battalions go to Ulster either as one of the garrison units in which case their tour lasts two years (previously eighteen months) or as a 'roulement' unit for $4\frac{1}{2}$ months. Typical of one of these tours was the four months' tour completed by the 3rd Battalion the Royal Green Jackets (3 RGJ) in Belfast in 1973. The battalion took over responsibility for operations on 26th July. Battalion HQ was housed in the Springfield Road Police Station; A Company found themselves in the old Administrative Annexe of the Royal Victoria Hospital and were responsible for the Iveagh, Beechmount, Cavendish and Collins districts; they were also responsible for guarding the Royal Victoria Hospital which included preventing attacks on injured soldiers and the escape of IRA prisoners under treatment. B Company was housed in the North Howard Street Mill whence they looked after the Clonard, a Republican stronghold, and the Protestant fringe of the Lower Shankill. R Company were in MacRory Park, a camp completely constructed of 'Portakabins', and were responsible for the Rodney, St James and across the Falls Road to the Westrock and Whiterock. S Company was based in Vere Foster School and Henry Taggart Hall so that their responsibility was the notorious Ballymurphy, New Barnsley and Moyard Areas. The administrative elements of HQ Company were based in an old mill in Ligoniel in the north-west outskirts of Belfast. Finally A Company 1st Light Infantry, which was under command 3 RGJ, occupied Blackmountain School in the Protestant Highfield and Springmartin Estates.

3 RGJ area of responsibility conveniently covered most of the territory terrorized by the 2nd Provisional 'Battalion' of the

IRA. This organization until shortly before the arrival of 3 RGJ
had numbered about eight officers and thirty or more
volunteers but attrition by the army over the preceding months
had steadily reduced its numbers to a few high-ranking officers
and low grade juvenile volunteers. Such a process of attrition
had of course to be achieved by exclusively legal means.
However there were sufficient to produce enough snipers,
gunmen and bombers to make life unpleasant. 3 RGJ's first
incident occurred on the afternoon of 28th July when a foot
patrol was fired at by more than one gunman from a range of
about a hundred yards. A burst of automatic low-velocity fire
and several high-velocity shots missed the patrol but went
through the glass entrance door of some pensioners' flats. A
few days later an S Company patrol from the Anti-Tank
Platoon noticed a young woman in New Barnsley with a
somewhat curious gait. On closer examination her discomfort
was found to be caused by a .303 sniper rifle complete with
telescopic sight. Two days later the familiar marzipan-like
smell of explosive led another patrol to search a derelict house
where they uncovered one rifle, a revolver, assorted
ammunition and a quantity of explosives. This seemed to open
the flood gates so that by the last week in August various finds
netted eighteen weapons including a Soviet manufactured
RPG-7 Rocket launcher and 2,600 rounds of ammunition.

Then on the last day of August 3 RGJ shot the infamous
PIRA terrorist Jim Bryson. It is worth examining this incident
in some detail. Bryson who came from a fiercely Republican
family had acquired a reputation with the RUC for bullying
and brawling during his youth. He grew into a squat,
broad-shouldered evil-looking man who readily joined the
IRA to indulge his homicidal tendencies when the troubles
started in 1969. During the escalation of the insurrection in
Belfast in 1971 Bryson developed into a cunning and ruthless
terrorist. He operated mainly in the Ballymurphy area where
his crude leadership and shooting exploits made him into
something of a cult hero. In June 1972 he took command of
the Ballymurphy Provisional Company. He ruled it and the
people of the Ballymurphy by a system of terror which
demanded and received universal obedience. He was also
extremely active himself and is believed to have murdered a
number of soldiers and policemen personally with his Armalite

rifle fitted with a telescopic sight. He was arrested in November 1972 but escaped from the Crumlin Road Court House in March 1973. He fled to Eire but was asked by the Provisional Brigade Staff to return to the Ballymurphy in August to help redress the balance against the Official IRA whose influence had been growing in the area. He immediately started to terrorize the local Official IRA men who decided that Bryson would have to be executed. Such was the degree of mutual distrust among the IRA in the Ballymurphy on 31st August.

On the morning of the same day an S Company corporal and a rifleman climbed stealthily into the attic of a flat directly overlooking a circle of open ground surrounded by council houses known as the Bullring. A hole in the roof, caused by some missing tiles, afforded them a good view of the Bullring and the roads leading off it. This was part of a pattern of three or four Observation Posts or OPs that S Company maintained to collect tactical intelligence and maintain general surveillance over the area. Soldiers would stay in the OPs for several days on end whereupon, if the position had not been compromised, they would be relieved by another team.

At 1830 hours that evening it was the corporal's turn on duty. He was bored and had seen nothing of interest all day. He noticed an olive green Hillman Hunter approaching the Bullring. Suddenly to his astonishment he saw three rifles sticking out of the window. Before he could do much the car drove off out of sight. He reported on his radio to Company HQ all he had seen. Moments later another OP reported on the radio net that the car was continuing to cruise around the area followed by a red van. It subsequently transpired that what in fact was happening was that Bryson accompanied by three notorious PIRA terrorists Paddy Mulvenna, ex-adjutant and commander of the Ballymurphy Company, 'Bimbo' O'Rawe and Frank Duffy were driving round the Ballymurphy partly to demonstrate their disregard for the Army and partly to humiliate the Officials.

The Hillman followed by the red van reappeared in the Bullring, motored slowly around it and then stopped at a junction some fifty yards beyond. The occupants got out and Bryson began to direct them to ambush positions. The corporal carefully moved one of the tiles in front of him to one side so as to get a better view and to create a cramped fire position for himself. As he did so he inadvertently dislodged a tile which clattered down on to the ground alerting the ambush party to his presence, one of whom fired in the general direction of the OP. The corporal immediately fired four rounds although he could scarcely aim in his cramped position. He was forced to pull his rifle in when it developed a stoppage. In the interval which followed Bryson and his gang made good their escape in the cars for when the corporal looked again the road was empty. Their position now compromised, the corporal and the rifleman set about enlarging the hole by kicking more tiles out. The corporal stuck his head out to try and get a better view and withdrew it sharply as two rounds hit the roof. He fired three quick rounds at a gunman he glimpsed but missed.

Thinking that the gunmen were now making good their escape both soldiers hurriedly prepared to leave their OP. As they were doing so, the corporal was amazed to see the Hillman returning to the same junction. Ironically Bryson had become confused by the problem that had faced so many British soldiers in Belfast, that of determining where the fire had come from. In built-up areas it is virtually impossible to tell from which direction a shot is fired, the 'crack and thump' of a high-velocity round echoing and re-echoing off the walls of the tightly knit Belfast streets. Bryson thinking he was driving into danger had thrown his car into a wild 'U' turn. As they came back into view the corporal fired at the accelerating Hillman trying to incapacitate it before it reached the corner. The first rounds hit O'Rawe in the shoulder and catapulted him from the back seat into the front of the car. Then a 7.62-mm round entered the back of Bryson's neck. As he slumped forward the car careered into the small front garden of 99 Ballymurphy Road. The corporal and rifleman watched the car crash some two hundred yards away and took the opportunity to jump down from the OP in the attic to the flat below where they took up fire positions to cover the car.

Mulvenna was the first to recover; he flung open the door of the car and rolled on to the ground from where he engaged the OP with his Armalite. Duffy also began to fire from the back of the car with an MI carbine. Mulvenna then decided to make a run for it. As he did so the corporal fired three shots, two of which hit, and Mulvenna died instantly. The next to go was

Bimbo O'Rawe who, though wounded, was still clutching a Garand as he ran towards the front door of 99 Ballymurphy Road. Again the corporal fired three shots hitting O'Rawe as he pitched forward inside the house. He then turned his attention to Duffy who was firing wildly as he sprinted away down the road. The corporal fired but missed.

When S Company patrols arrived they found Mulvenna dead, Bryson unconscious and O'Rawe badly wounded. Bryson died three weeks later. In the follow-up thirteen rifles and pistols and large quantities of ammunition and explosives were found. The perseverance, alertness and good shooting of S Company had rid Ulster of three heartless murderers. In all that August six gunmen were killed bringing the total number of terrorists put out of action in one way or another to 2,265 including 195 Protestants. In Belfast the three Provisional battalions ceased to exist. In their place the Provisionals created small 'Active Service Units' (ASUs) based on the Communist cell system whereby members would be known only to others in the same unit, and whose commanders would be directly responsible to the Belfast Commander, Ivor Bell. Ironically the Provisionals were convinced that Bryson had been eliminated by the Officials; no one had of course seen from where the shots had come. Soldiers only appeared on the scene after the event. It suited the Army to perpetuate the myth.

The remainder of the 3 RGJ tour was equally eventful. There were more shootings and several bomb explosions including one car bomb of some 450lb of explosive which slightly injured two Green Jacket soldiers. An A Company patrol successfully wounded a sniper who habitually shot at sentries in McRory Park base from the City Cemetery. Blood trails confirmed the hit. Finally on 28th November the battalion returned to England. Compared to many of the tours in 1971/72 it had been quiet. But it was very typical of the countless tours that have now been undertaken by every major unit in the British Army: four months of continuous activity, of eighteen-hour days, of constant patrolling and unrelenting tension; nights spent in cramped accommodation in bunk beds or perhaps days and nights on end in an OP in a derelict building; the real danger from bullet and bomb; the hatred of bigots but also the gratitude of the vast majority; four months of this and the strain showed. The statistics for the 3 RGJ tour are at Table 1.

The experiment in Direct Rule from Westminster ended on 31st December 1973, having been imposed in March the previous year. The Sunningdale Agreement of 9th December 1973 produced a power-sharing formula that would involve representatives of all sections of the community in a new Executive to replace the old Assembly. On 23rd January 1974 the Loyalists walked out of Stormont. The political in-fighting worsened until on 15th May the Ulster Workers Council called a General Strike with the purpose of forcing the British Government to shelve the Sunningdale Agreement and the power-sharing Executive. The strike was chillingly effective and demonstrated clearly that, without the support of the majority, the power-sharing Executive could not get off the ground. Direct rule was resumed in June.

Meanwhile the process of slowly handing over control to the RUC was starting. At the time of Operation Motorman there were 21,000 British troops in Ulster. By July 1974 this had been reduced to 15,000. The pace did not lessen however in South Armagh which became known in the press as 'The Murder Triangle'. Fortunately at an early stage in the campaign the army had set up bases at Crossmaglen, Newtownhamilton, Forkhill, Bessbrook and other border towns. In view of the increasing violence in the area the 3rd Battalion the Light Infantry and a company of paratroopers were flown to Northern Ireland in September 1975 to join the 3rd Battalion the Royal Regiment of Fusiliers who were already operating from these bases. South Armagh had always been a Republican stronghold and it was easy for the Provisionals to operate from such towns as Dundalk across the border. The border itself meanders through fields and hedgerows. It is difficult to know precisely where it runs let alone guard it or block it in any way. The army has always been the first to admit that the IRA can cross the border almost at will. It would take defences such as those that exist between East and West Germany to seal the border effectively. Clearly this is not a practical or desirable solution between two democratic and friendly states. It soon became far too dangerous for the army to operate in vehicles in the border area; the distinctive whine of an armoured vehicle can be heard miles away and makes an easy target for a remotely detonated mine in the narrow winding lanes. Instead soldiers move stealthily on foot or by helicopter. The base at Crossmaglen is still exclusively supplied by helicopter except for occasional heavily escorted and picqueted convoys bringing in heavy plant and equipment. In January 1976 the SAS were deployed in the Province since when they have used their special surveillance techniques and ability to survive in the open in all types of weather for long periods to contribute towards the reduction of violence in the area.

The diary of violence continued through 1975 and into 1976. Table 2 provides a summary. It was on 10th August 1976 that a landrover patrol of the King's Own Border Regiment gave chase to a Ford Cortina motor car carrying two gunmen who were escaping from a shooting incident in which they had opened fire on troops of the same regiment minutes earlier. As the landrover chased the car an Armalite was seen to be pointed rearwards from a window of the car. The patrol fired four shots. Seconds later the car swerved out of control, mounted the pavement and ran down a mother and her three children. The mother was injured and the children killed. As the patrol drew up at the scene of the accident one of the gunmen attempted to fire. He was shot and wounded. The driver was found to be dead from gunshot wounds. It was as a result of this horrific incident that the Northern Ireland Peace Movement was formed by Mairead Corrigan, an aunt of the dead children, and Betty Williams. Though the organization is now moribund it played an important part for nearly two years in uniting moderate men and women of both communities in a demonstration of their revulsion of the continuing violence.

Members of the Peace Movement were intimidated and harassed which only encouraged them to continue their work. The gradual return to normal life in recent years undoubtedly owes much to these two brave women and the movement which they started, not to mention the tragic sacrifice of Mr and Mrs Maguire, the parents of the dead children. In October 1977 it was announced that the leaders of the Peace Movement had been awarded the 1976 Nobel Peace Prize.

Although by 1977 there had been great reductions in the overall level of violence in the Province, particularly as regards casualties among the security forces, the vicious inter-sectarian violence continued unabated. Although they had existed before, the Protestant paramilitary Ulster Defence Association (UDA) and other even more extreme organizations such as the Ulster Volunteer Force (UVF) and Ulster Freedom Fighters (UFF) gained a new-found confidence after the 1974 Ulster Workers Council Strike. Tit-for-tat killings and maimings by the Provisionals and the Protestant paramilitary groups and the rival warfare between the Provisionals and Officials have tended to account for an increasing number of total casualties the more the Security Forces get on top of the situation. One of the more dramatic killings was the murder on 28th October 1976 of Maire Drumm, a leading Sinn Fein activist, as she lay in her bed in the Mater Hospital in Belfast. Two days in May 1977 will serve as an example of sectarian violence in Ulster: on 10th May a Protestant bus driver was shot dead at the wheel of his bus in Belfast. Later the same day the body of a Catholic was found in the garden of a derelict house. Then on 12th May Mr Douglas Deering who owned a small supermarket in Rosslea County Fermanagh and who was a local Justice of the Peace was shot dead at work. He was a Protestant. The same day terrorists fired four shots at a petrol- tanker driver who was driving his vehicle through East Belfast – fortunately they missed. During two days in July 1977 four members of the OIRA were shot by PIRA assassination squads and a further sixteen people were seriously injured in gun battles or assassination attempts. Two of these were boys aged thirteen and fifteen, one of whom had been 'kneecapped' while the other had gunshot wounds to his chest. Where murder is considered inappropriate the punishment of 'kneecapping' is popular; this consists of blowing one or both of the kneecaps off an offender by shooting at them at close range. Such is the mentality of the men of violence in Northern Ireland.

In November 1977 Lt-General Sir David House was replaced as GOC Northern Ireland by Lt-General Tim Creasey. Creasey was chosen to oversee the gradual handing back of responsibility for security to the RUC, a process that continues to this day.

On February 1978 an OP of the 2nd Battalion the Royal Green Jackets in South Armagh came under fire from across the border with the Republic. The Commanding Officer, Lt-Colonel Iain Cordon-Lloyd, and the Close Observation

Platoon commander, Captain Philip Schofield, flew to the scene in a Gazelle helicopter to assess the situation and provide assistance if possible. As the helicopter banked at low level the pilot momentarily lost control killing Cordon-Lloyd and seriously injuring Schofield. The loss of Lt-Colonel Cordon-Lloyd was of course a tragedy for his family and friends but at the same time the army lost one of its most promising young commanding officers who many say was destined for much greater things. During the same tour 2 RGJ lost Rifleman Smith who was killed while removing a booby-trapped tricolour from a telegraph pole. Sergeant Bennett was also severely wounded in the head when a device was detonated by a command wire which ran across the border. Though he fought valiantly to recover and was given much encouragement by his regiment he failed after two years to reach an acceptable medical standard. A dedicated soldier, Sergeant Bennett is only one of many who have been forced through injury to leave his chosen career and seek employment in civilian life.

The following August a command-detonated mine killed eighteen mostly Parachute Regiment soldiers who were travelling in the back of a 4-ton truck along a main road adjacent to the border and close to the village of Warrenpoint. As the incident had occurred in his area of responsibility Lt-Colonel David Blair, Commanding Officer of the Queen's Own Highlanders, landed by helicopter to assess the situation. He ran from the helicopter towards the side of the road whereupon the terrorists watching the scene from across the border detonated a second device which immediately killed Blair. So close was he to the explosion that his remains have never been found. In the same week Earl Mountbatten of Burma was killed in Eire while on a fishing trip in his boat with members of his family. The death of Earl Mountbatten in Eire and the holocaust at Warrenpoint stunned the nation and the world.

The period 1980–84 has in contrast been relatively quiet. The troop level is down to 10,500 and looks like being reduced further. The RUC are increasingly in the forefront of the battle against the terrorists. Routine security is now very much the responsibility of the police. In most cases the army is only called out in reaction to an incident. While it would be a

Table 1

3 RGJ Statistics 1973 Tour

Casualties:

IRA killed	2
Wounded	1+1 possible
3 RGJ killed	Nil
Wounded	Nil (Hospitalized)

Arrests:

Serious Criminal Charges:

Arms/Ammunition and Explosives	41
Attempted Murder, Membership IRA	22
Leading to interim Custody orders	25

Minor Criminal Charges:

Rioting, Assault	132

Finds:

Rifles	23
Sub Machine Guns	3
Rocket Launchers	1
Pistols	18
Miscellaneous (air rifles etc)	6
Total	51 weapons

Ammunition:	10,069 rounds
Explosives	105 lbs
Nail, Blast, Petrol, Mortar Bombs, RPG 7 Rockets	10

Shooting Incidents:

At the Battalion	272
By the Battalion	244

foolish man who forecast that the end was in sight, things are undoubtedly looking brighter. The gunmen are increasingly isolated and no longer have the active or passive support of a large section of the Catholic community.

Nevertheless, the IRA has continued throughout 1983 and even into 1984 to mount regular terrorist attacks against the security forces and civilian population. The emphasis during this period has been against the UDR and RUC often during their off-duty hours. Twenty-seven members of the UDR and RUC were murdered during November 1983 alone. The Harrods' bombing of December 1983 demonstrated not only the ability of the IRA to mount such an operation but also their determination to continue their campaign by whatever means they deem necessary. Within the current 'rules of the game' it would be difficult for the army and police to reduce the level of violence any further than has presently been achieved. Unless conditions of a police state are imposed the terrorist can operate with relative ease; there is a limit to what can be achieved by military means alone. The security forces' role is inevitably reactive. It is perhaps in the intelligence field that hope lies. If terrorists can be identified and their organizations infiltrated then there is a greater chance of sufficient evidence being secured for the purpose of conviction. A purely military victory in Ireland is not possible. The Army must continue however, to keep the level of violence as low as possible to allow other influences to work. And there are hopeful signs that this is happening.

The Emergency in Northern Ireland 1969-84 has been a tragic episode in the history of the United Kingdom. It was probably inevitable given the incredible attitudes of successive Ulster Governments to the Catholic minority in the post-war years. The speeches from Stormont's Hansard are breath-taking in their bald sectarianism: the Minister for Labour answers a written question at one point; it was totally untrue that out of thirty-one porters at Stormont twenty-eight were Roman Catholics; this was nothing but a smear. 'There are thirty Protestants and one Roman Catholic, and the Roman Catholic is only temporary.' Even Prime Minister Terence O'Neill, who some Loyalists thought far too liberal, said in Canada in the 1960s: 'It is frightfully hard to explain to Protestants that if you give Roman Catholics a good job and a

TABLE 2
The Northern Ireland Campaign – General Statistics

	1969	1970	1971	19
Terrorist Incidents				
Bombs		170	1515	18.
Incendiaries				
Shootings		213	1756	106.
Casualties				
Regular Army killed			43	1(
UDR killed			5	:
RUC killed	1	2	11	
Civilians killed	10	16	61	2:
Terrorists Killed				
Republican	2	7	52	(
Loyalist			2	
Finds				
Weapons		324	717	12(
Explosives (tons)		0.4	2.6	27
Terrorists Charged				
Loyalist and Republican				5:

1973	1974	1975	1976	1977
1520	1113	635	1192	535
	270	56	239	611
5018	3206	1803	1908	1081
58	28	14	14	15
8	7	6	15	14
13	15	11	23	14
128	145	196	223	59
38	16	10	22	6
4	5	10		4
1595	1260	825	837	590
31.6	23.7	9.9	16.9	2.7
1414	1367	1196	1276	1308

	1978	1979	1980
Terrorist Incidents			
Bombs	633	564	421
Incendiaries	115	60	2
Shootings	755	728	642
Casualties			
Regular Army killed	14	38	8
UDR killed	7	10	9
RUC killed	10	14	9
Civilians killed	43	48	44
Terrorists Killed			
Republican	7	3	3
Loyalist			2
Finds			
Weapons	400	301	203
Explosives (tons)	3.5	2.9	3.6
Terrorists Charged			
Loyalist and Republican	843	670	671

1981	1982	1983	1984 (Up to 27 Jan '84)
530	332	367	24
49	36	43	–
1142	547	424	12
10	21	5	–
13	7	10	2
21	12	18	1
52	50	37	–
15	7	6	–
–	–	1	–
398	321	199	32
7.57	5.60	5.11	.42
918	686	613	49

good house they will live like perfectly decent Protestants.'
Out of this bigotry grew the Civil Rights Movement which
created a perfect wagon for the IRA band.

The past fifteen years has been agony for Ireland and, as
the violence has spilled over on to the mainland, for the rest of
the United Kingdom too. The Emergency has of course
affected the army as much as it has the people of Northern
Ireland. It is a source of wonder to the British and to
foreigners alike how the army in Ulster continues to deal so
impartially and patiently with a seemingly insoluble situation.
Trying to keep the peace between two warring communities is
no enviable task particularly when one is in the firing line. It is
all the more difficult when they are one's fellow citizens. It is
even more difficult when the normal process of law and order
has broken down. The soldiers in Northern Ireland have
become policemen, welfare workers, male nurses, detectives,
marriage-guidance counsellors, petrol-pump attendants,
prison wardens, civil servants, furniture-removal agencies,
farmworkers, and above all else a military version of the
Citizens' Advice Bureau. It is doubtful whether any other army
could have risen to the occasion. The United Kingdom owes an
immense debt of gratitude to all those who have served in
Northern Ireland. The *Financial Times* art critic, when reviewing
an exhibition of painting of the Ulster troubles, said it all:
'The soldier is a professional, and whatever the rights and
wrongs of the different views in Northern Ireland, now
inextricably mixed, the soldier is there – not at war, but warred
upon ... I do think, with all due respect to the awful
complexities of what has happened and is happening in
Northern Ireland, we are and should be immensely and
publicly proud of the Army. To me it is astonishing that in this
unofficial, sporadic civil war carried out not on battlefields and
beaches, but day to day in shops, streets, hotels, pubs, homes,
the Army, a perpetual target both physically and
psychologically, has managed with so few incidents.'

13

Dhofar
1970-76

Probably the most fascinating of all Britain's Brush Fire Wars is also the most recently concluded. The Dhofar campaign is certainly the least well known.

The harsh regime of Sultan Sa'ib bin Taimur, the thirteenth hereditary monarch of Oman, was particularly oppressive in Dhofar where he lived as a virtual recluse in his palace in Salalah. When oil was discovered in the Gulf States thousands of his subjects left to seek their fortune. Inevitably their contact with civilization in the oil-rich Gulf Emirates sowed the seeds of discontent which ultimately led to revolt. By 1960 the people had many grievances. There were no schools so Omanis who sought an education were forced to become political exiles. Some inevitably were lured to Russia or East Germany. There were no hospitals in Dhofar until 1970 and only one road inland from the coastal plain. There was no running water and no electricity. Certainly no Western habits or customs of any kind were permitted. All this might have been acceptable if only the Sultan had ruled more benevolently. Instead he instilled a dreadful fear in his people. However it must be said in his defence that his reason for holding back progress was to keep Western decadence – as he saw it – out of his country. He genuinely felt that his people would be better off in the long run without the so-called benefits of civilization.

Finally in 1965 the mountain tribesmen rose in revolt. Across the border in the Eastern Aden Protectorate and further west in Aden and the Radfan the British had been engaged in a bitter struggle with Arab Nationalists since 1963 (see Chapter

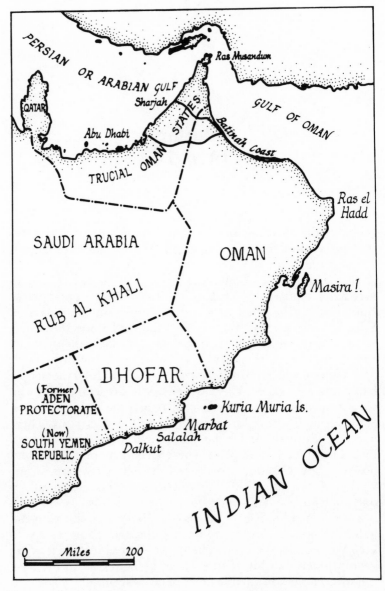

20 Dhofar's strategic position near the mouth of the Gulf of Oman

11). It was inevitable that the struggle should spread. At first the rebellion was little more than a nuisance; the Dhofari tribesmen engaged in a sporadic campaign of mine-laying and ambush. But the situation changed when the British left neighbouring Aden in 1967; the new Communist Government in what was now the People's Democratic Republic of Yemen (PDRY) provided a secure sanctuary and source of supply for the rebels. Moreover the Dhofari tribesmen's ethnic links were with the people of South Yemen. The avowed policy of the PDRY was to push up through Oman to grab the oil-rich Gulf States. The first stage of this policy was to take over the revolution in Dhofar. Many Dhofaris were trained in the PDRY and then returned armed with Soviet weaponry to indoctrinate others.

Dhofar provided an ideal situation for a guerilla uprising. The region is about the same size as Wales and, apart from a narrow coastal plain, is exclusively mountainous. The peaks rise to about 4,000 feet. The monsoon brings low cloud and rain to the Jebel between June and September; but because of scorching sunshine for the rest of the year, the luxurious growth of grass resulting from the monsoon only lasts a further two to four months. The lower slopes of the hills are precipitous making access to the Jebel from the plain difficult in the extreme. Caves and gullies abound. This belt of tropical vegetation and limestone caves varies between one and ten miles in depth. Beyond is the 'Empty Quarter'.

By 1970 it was clear that the Sultan would lose the war in Dhofar unless some fairly drastic steps were taken. A virtually bloodless palace coup planned by the Sultan's son and heir Qaboos and executed on 23rd July provided the opportunity for the change in direction that was needed. Sultan Qaboos opened his country to civil reform and overnight removed some of the worst excesses of his father's regime. But up in the Jebel the rising had gathered momentum and it was clear that nothing but military measures would defeat it. Fortunately petroleum revenues allowed the Sultan to undertake a substantial programme of expansion of the Sultan's Armed Forces (SAF). He also asked Great Britain for help. Within days of the coup the SAS were authorized by the new Heath Government to provide a small advisory team which produced a long-term plan to defeat the guerilla insurgency. It was based

upon the by now traditional British method of combining
military operations with a co-ordinated 'hearts and minds'
campaign to win over the sympathy of the people to the
Government cause. As in Malaya a vigorous campaign was
launched to encourage rebels to defect. An early success was
Mohammed Suhail, formerly a soldier in the Trucial Oman
Scouts who had become disillusioned with the previous regime
and joined the rebels. He was immediately co-opted to work
for the Sultan's Intelligence Staff. Between September 1970
and March 1971 a total of 201 rebels surrendered. By
December 1975 a further 800 had defected.

At first the SAS team in Salalah which consisted only of one
troop of fifteen men were restricted to intelligence, advisory
and community projects. The SAS therefore split themselves
into small two and three-man teams often accompanied by a
doctor or veterinary surgeon and worked among the people in
the villages along the coastal plain. Perhaps the most greatly
appreciated of their many projects was the drilling of water
wells. The work was usually carried out by civilian contractors
but as often as not instigated by the SAS. But as more of the
rebels defected an imperceptible shift in emphasis in the main
task of the SAS began to take place. In much the same way as
surrendered Mau Mau were formed into 'Pseudo-gangs' in
Kenya and surrendered enemy personnel (SEP) were used as
informers in the Malayan campaign, the rebel defectors were
reunited into anti-guerilla units known as 'firqas'. The
training, organization and leadership of these 'firqas' became
more and more the real reason for the presence of the SAS in
Dhofar.

While the SAS, now nearly at squadron strength, continued
their important work with the 'firqas', further contributions to
the military effort were made by both Britain and sympathetic
Arab leaders. British engineers completed invaluable military
and civil aid projects the latter being particularly appreciated
by the people. Royal Engineer assistance was provided under
the umbrella title of 'Operation Tenable'. For eight months
out of every year there was always an Engineer Squadron
Headquarters and two troops in Dhofar. Perhaps their greatest
feat was the construction of fifty-three kilometres of wire fence
and minefields christened the 'Hornbeam Line'. British pilots
were also employed to fly in the rapidly expanding Sultan of

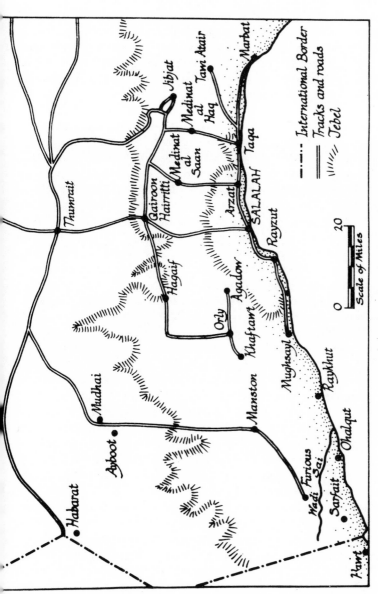

21   The area of operations in Dhofar 1970-76

Oman's Air Force (SOAF). The King of Jordan dispatched an infantry regiment to Dhofar in 1972 and the Shah of Iran 1,500 troops in 1973 with orders to take and keep open the only road between Salalah and Thumrait. Also numerous British officers were either seconded or on contract to SAF for two-year periods. Contract officers, though mostly ex-British Army officers, were hired as individuals by the Sultan and not loaned by the British Government.

But it was the SAS which made an impact in Dhofar out of all proportion to their limited numbers. The squadron was now deployed entirely with the 'firqas'. These small groups of SAS men were involved in many skirmishes with the rebels but undoubtedly the most ferocious and desperate battle fought by the SAS in Dhofar was the Battle of Marbat on 18th July 1972. The story is worth telling in some detail because it illustrates so perfectly the type of action in which the British Army has been involved so often and so regularly between 1945 and 1983 and which, although limited in size and scope and often seemingly of little consequence at the time, have had far-reaching effects upon the development of nations.

Marbat was situated on the coast forty miles east of Salalah; the settlement consisted of a few flat-topped houses and two mud-built forts. The whole was surrounded by a perimeter wire in the north and east and on the other two sides by the sea. The Jebel rose massively only one and a half miles to the north. Marbat was garrisoned by twenty-five men of the Dhofar Gendarmerie armed with Belgian FN semi-automatic rifles who resided in a fort situated in the north-east corner of the town and only about 150 metres from the perimeter fence. In front of the fort was a gunpit which housed an ancient but perfectly serviceable 25-pounder artillery piece which was normally used to put down harassing fire on the rebels in the Jebel. Also in Marbat was the local 'firqa' with an effective strength on 18th July of about thirty men. They too were armed with FN rifles and some light machine-guns. Finally in the other fort in the north-west corner of the town were thirty Askari warriors from northern Oman armed with bolt-action .303 rifles; they were in the nature of a private army owing allegiance to the Wali or Sultan's representative in Marbat. In addition to this garrison, the effective strength of which was probably about sixty-five men, was the British Army Training

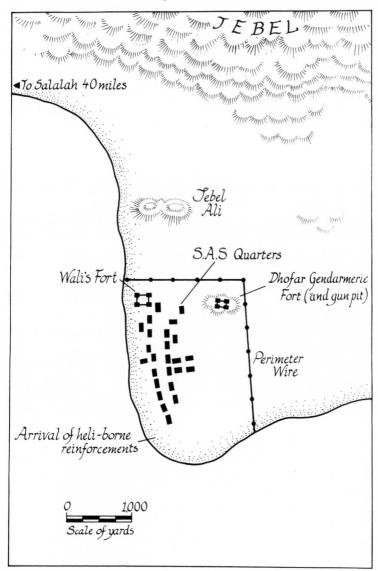

22   The Battle of Marbat, 19th July 1972

Team at Marbat consisting of ten SAS soldiers commanded by
Captain Mike Kealy. In addition to their personal weapons the
SAS had at their disposal one .5-inch Browning machine-gun
and an 81-mm mortar. They were quartered in a building
situated roughly half way between the two forts.

It was against this garrison that the Marxist guerillas of the
Dhofar Liberation Front had decided to make their most
audacious attack of the war. They had managed to assemble
some 250 tribesmen armed mostly with Kalashnikov AK-47
assault rifles but also with various machine-guns, two 75-mm
anti-tank guns of Russian manufacture, a Swedish 84-mm Carl
Gustav rocket launcher and a formidable array of light and
medium mortar support.

At 5.30 in the morning the garrison in the town was alerted
by the sound of rifle fire from the Jebel Ali some 1,000 metres
to the north of the town; it soon became clear that the
gendarmerie piquet there had been overrun and that accurate
fire from a rebel machine-gun was now emanating from the
Jebel Ali. At the same time groups of rebels could be seen
skirmishing towards the perimeter fence in the area of the
Gendarmerie Fort but also further to the south so that the
town was now completely surrounded.

Kealy ordered his radio operator to inform Army
Headquarters in Salalah of their predicament and then
proceeded to get on with the business of directing the battle.
The situation did not look at all good. His forces were heavily
outnumbered and, except for the 25-pounder which was not
really suitable for close-quarter fighting, heavily outgunned.
Nevertheless the SAS men, who were still fighting from their
quarters on the northern edge of the town, put down a
tremendous weight of fire on the enemy positions with the
Browning and the mortar, while two other SAS men, Corporal
Labalaba and Trooper Ti – both from Fiji – and an Omani
gunner, Walid Khamis, manned the 25-pounder in the gunpit
by the Gendarmerie Fort.

By 7 am the rebels had breached the wire in several places
and were perilously close to the gunpit. 84-mm Carl Gustav
and RPG-7 rockets were being fired at close range at the
Gendarmerie Fort, the mud walls of which were progressively
collapsing under the weight of fire. The only thing that was
preventing the group of rebels now consolidated some thirty

metres from the gunpit from physically occupying it was the devastatingly accurate fire co-ordinated by an SAS corporal in the SAS living quarters. What was desperately needed now was air support from SOAF but the cloud base was so low – a factor which must have prompted the rebels to attack in the midst of the monsoon season in July – that air support appeared to be out of the question. Kealy had in fact already asked for the Strikemasters in Salalah to stand by to provide support if at all possible.

During a brief lull in the battle Kealy decided to join his men in the gunpit; he knew that some of them were wounded. Accompanied by his medical orderly he proceeded to make a daring dash across the open ground to the fort and gunpit. On reaching his destination Kealy discovered that both the Fijian SAS men were wounded but still fighting and that Walid Khamis, the Omani gunner, was seriously wounded. A gendarme lay dead on the parapet. Though wounded Corporal Labalaba was loading and firing the 25-pounder at point-blank range over open sights unaided. In desperation Kealy called for an airstrike. As he did so the courageous Corporal Labalaba was shot dead and his medical orderly badly wounded. With only Trooper Ti and himself now left defending the gunpit, Kealy prayed for a miracle. It came in the shape of two Strikemaster jet aircraft flying at 450 knots about fifty feet above ground level and even then only just beneath the cloud base. There was no shortage of targets; the pilots strafed the guerillas along the perimeter fence with their machine-guns and dropped 500-lb bombs on groups of guerillas threatening the Gendarmerie Fort.

The arrival of the aircraft turned the tide and indeed some of the guerillas had begun to withdraw in the face of the air attack when at 9.15 am a party of eighteen SAS men landed by helicopter on the beach at the south-western corner of the town. Their arrival put the outcome of the battle beyond any doubt but it was not until 10.30 am that the most seriously wounded could be evacuated by helicopter and not until midday that the situation was fully under control again. The guerillas knew when they were beaten and melted away into the Jebel.

The arrival of the SAS reinforcements was perhaps the greatest stroke of luck of all. The day that the Dhofar

Liberation Front had selected for their attack happened to be the day when the men of B Squadron 22 Special Air Service Regiment were due to be relieved after a three-month tour of duty in Marbat by a group from G Squadron who had arrived in Salalah the previous day. When Kealy's radio message first alerted Army Headquarters in Salalah of the rebel attack the men of G Squadron were already preparing to fly to Marbat. Had the rebels attacked on any other day reinforcements would not have been available so quickly and the outcome could have been very different.

B Squadron lost Corporal Labalaba and Trooper Tobin, Kealy's medical orderly, both of whom died of gunshot wounds. Apart from Walid Khamis, the Omani artilleryman, the only other fatality among the defenders of Marbat was a gendarme. The guerillas sustained thirty fatal casualties and probably approaching eighty of their number were wounded. The blow dealt not only to their numbers but also to their pride prevented the guerillas from ever again putting such a sizeable force into the field.

Kealy* was awarded the Distinguished Service Order and two of his men a Military Cross and Military Medal apiece. Trooper Tobin was posthumously awarded a Distinguished Conduct Medal and Corporal Labalaba was also posthumously Mentioned in Despatches.

There were many other battles in which casualties among the Security Forces were far more serious and in which larger formations of troops were involved but the action at Marbat epitomized the sort of engagement in which the British soldier excels. It is a wonderful tale of derring-do. It encapsulates in one day in July 1972 the phenomenon of post-1945 British Brush Fire Wars.

Despite the success at Marbat the war in Dhofar ground on. In 1974–5 a further eleven British soldiers were killed, two of whom died when their Jetranger helicopter was shot down by small-arms fire, and more were wounded. Typical of the gallantry shown by so many was the action of Captain Simon Garthwaite of the SAS who was killed on 12th April 1974 while trying to rescue a 'firqa' patrol pinned down by enemy fire. In many ways more remarkable than the SAS officers who served

* Major Mike Kealy subsequently died from exposure during an SAS exercise on the Brecon Beacons in 1977.

in Dhofar were the officers from the ordinary regiments of the line who volunteered for secondment to SAF normally for a period of two years. One such as this was Major Timothy Edward Fox Taylor was was killed earlier in the campaign on 7th November 1971. He had joined the first Green Jackets, the 43rd and 52nd, in 1963 when the battalion had been in Borneo. In September 1970 he was seconded to SAF. He had turned down the chance to go to Nigeria because Muscat would give him an independent command and more active service. In June 1971 his Brigade Commander wrote to his parent regiment: 'You will, I know, be pleased to hear that Major T.E.F. Taylor, who is a Company Commander in the Desert Regiment of SAF, has recently been awarded The Sultan's Commendation. This is the equivalent of a Mention in Despatches. Tim won it for his excellent planning and exemplary conduct in a series of major operations in Dhofar shortly after he joined SAF. Tim is clearly a very promising commander and leader of men, and it is significant that he won this award so soon after joining us. I expect great things of him in the months to come and am delighted to have him in the Force. The Desert Regiment has a long, hard slog in Dhofar; they are back in the Northern Oman now but will return to the Dhofar battlefields in October. Please let Tim's colleagues at home know about his award as I am sure he is too modest to tell them himself.'

In November he wrote: 'Tim was killed by a shell which burst on top of the protective stone wall (sangar) surrounding his tent. The enemy have been doing a certain amount of mortaring and 75-mm artillery shelling of the Desert Regiment's base in the Western Jebel in Dhofar: it is a real tragedy that Tim should have been the first chap killed in this way. He was a very good, resolute and sound officer; extremely respected and popular with all ranks, pink-and-brown faced. Only a few days before his death he had personally commanded an ambush action south-west of the base in which certainly eight, probably twelve, of the enemy were killed without loss to Tim's men.'

At the time of Taylor's death only a handful of people in Britain knew of British involvement in Dhofar. Most of those who were aware of the campaign were not exactly sure where Dhofar was. The villagers of Newnham-on-Severn,

Gloucestershire, where Timothy Taylor's family lived, were not very sure either. But then he was not the sort of person who wanted a fuss made. Total casualties during the 1971–75 period are put at 187 killed and 559 wounded of which 24 and 55 respectively were British.

In March 1974 a line of mines and barbed wire known as the 'Hornbeam Line' was built inland for fifty-three kilometres from the coast and some ninety kilometres from the border with South Yemen, an outstanding feat of engineering by Royal Engineers and some Jordanian engineers working under the protection of an Omani battalion for an entire year. One of the Royal Engineer Squadrons working on the 'Hornbeam Line' was commanded by a youthful Major Blashford-Snell.*

The effect of this line was to restrict supplies from reaching the guerillas in the central and eastern areas of Dhofar. Operations were then accelerated in the Jebel north and north-east of Salalah so that by May 1975 the rebels had been pushed back to a narrow strip adjacent to the South Yemen border. Although up to four companies of PDRY regulars had been operating inside Dhofar in support of the rebels up to mid-1974 their enthusiasm for fighting other people's battles had by October 1975 been exhausted.

By December the most serious cross-border traffic was the 85-mm, 122-mm and 130-mm artillery which the rebels still fired at the rate of 100 rounds per day. These were not particularly effective; the 120,000 rounds which were fired into Dhofar during 1972–5 caused less than ten fatalities. The real end of the campaign came in October 1975 when the Muscat Regiment commanded by Lt-Colonel Ian Christie broke out of an air-supplied mountain-top position at Sarfait on the Jebel and in the subsequent advance captured and held a three-mile-wide corridor to the sea thus finally cutting off the last escape and supply route to the south.

The Sarfait base had been captured in April 1972 in a daring helicopter-borne operation. A tactically important mountain top only five miles from the border was successfully secured without any opposition. Although the SAF Battalion held the mountain they were in fact unable to dominate the supply route in dead ground below. They were not strong enough to

---

* Later to become Colonel Blashford-Snell of Blue Nile Expedition fame.

break out and could not be reinforced because SOAF never owned more than twelve helicopters and it was all they could do to re-supply the troops already on the position. Even water had to be ferried in. Withdrawal would have dealt a dreadful blow to the prestige of SAF so they stayed at Sarfait, virtually powerless to affect the outcome of the war, for three and a half years until their breakout in October 1975 finally won the war.

Earlier that year in August a highly significant event had taken place. Brigadier Akehurst* had been visiting a SAF position near the border when ten Katushka rockets struck the position in quick succession. The normal form in the event of enemy rocket or mortar fire was to call for Strikemaster support. This was done, the planes rocketed the enemy positions and then turned for home. Just as Akehurst was returning to the SAF command post he heard an explosion, turned and saw a Strikemaster falling out of the sky about three miles away. As he watched the second jet was fired at but missed by what was clearly a missile as the smoke trail could be seen. At the same time a red-and-white parachute appeared in the sky signifying the successful ejection of the pilot from the aircraft downed by a Soviet SAM 7 surface-to-air missile. The operators had in fact been trained in Russia. Fortunately a helicopter was in the vicinity and was immediately directed to search for the ejected pilot. Despite small-arms fire and at least one further SAM 7 the pilot continued to descend to pick up the downed pilot which he eventually managed by using his winch. The helicopter which already had ten soldiers on board then climbed painfully slowly away. It was not fired at again and it must be assumed the SAM operator had run out of missiles. The bravery of the pilot was quite exceptional.

In all during the campaign twenty-three SAM 7s were fired. In addition to the Strikemaster one helicopter was shot down which had been flying at 10,000 feet. Certainly it made flying in Dhofar a dangerous business.

The final rebel-occupied village of Dalkut was taken on 1st December 1975. A few days later Akehurst reported to the Sultan that Dhofar was secure for civil development. Within twenty-four hours of the taking of Dalkut by SAF, food, clothes and paint for the neglected mosque were flown in. Teams of

---

* Now Major-General Akehurst, Commandant of the Staff College.

engineers set about sinking water wells and building schools.
The new Sultan was determined not to make the same mistakes
as his father. Indeed by late 1976 there were fourteen schools
in Dhofar including a boarding-school for orphan boys whose
fathers were killed in the fighting. These did not spring up
overnight. The process had been very similar to that in Malaya.
As an area was declared 'white' the civil development agencies
moved in; a track would be driven through to the newly
liberated area, a company would be left to protect the location,
a water well would be drilled and a mosque, clinic, school and
shop constructed. Finally the 'firqa' would be left to look after
the newly acquired territory and generally they told the enemy
to push off and not interfere with a good thing. No Dhofari
rebel who surrendered was punished; indeed many were
elevated to positions of national importance.

The Dhofar war was a unique victory by the forces of
counter-insurgency. The army was commanded by
Major-General Tim Creasey* from 1973 to 1975 and latterly
by Major-General Perkins; the Dhofar Brigade was
commanded by Brigadier Jack Fletcher from 1972 to 1974 and
then by Brigadier John Akehurst from 1974 to the end of the
war in 1976. The Dhofar Brigade consisted of:

> Twenty-four Armoured cars (SALADINS mounting
> 76-mm guns)
> Imperial Iranian Task Force (1500 troops)
> Five Battalions (two Omani, two Baluch with about
> twelve British officers each plus three independent
> companies)
> Forty guns (5.5-inch, 25-pounders, 105-mm howitzers,
> 4.2-inch mortars and 120-mm US mortars
> Three Engineer Squadrons
> SAS Squadron
> Signals Support

The SAF was officered half by British officers on secondment
from the British Army and half by contract officers, mostly
British but some from other Commonwealth countries; the
contribution by the Royal Engineers was vitally important but
that of the SAS in their training of the 'firqa' was perhaps the

---

* Now General Sir Tim Creasey Commander Sultan of Oman's Land
Forces (SOLF).

most vital of all. This is not to say the British won the war unaided. Far from it. The thousands of Iranian, Jordanian and Omani soldiers who provided the manpower to cut guerilla supply lines to the South Yemen were equally vital, as indeed were the 'firqas'. It was a remarkable victory that brought the Government from the verge of complete collapse in 1970 to outstanding success in 1976. Seldom has Communist-inspired insurgency been so roundly defeated. Undoubtedly the contribution of the British Army to this surprisingly under-publicized war was a very special one.

Sultan Qaboos told the ecstatic crowd which packed Muscat Stadium for his victory speech, 'Oman is the first Arab country to defeat international Communism on the battlefield. Therefore the Communists will not forget; they will adopt new methods and techniques. Everyone should be on the alert, the soldier on the battlefield, the farmer on his farm, even Ministers in their Departments.' Certainly the Sultan has ensured that the country is militarily prepared: SAF now numbers 14,000 men and even the Navy is 400 strong. The army is equipped with modern equipment including armoured cars and anti-tank guided weapons. SOAF is equipped with Jaguars, Strikemasters and Hunters as well as Rapier anti-aircraft missiles. SAF and SOAF contract officers are still mainly British. The threat from the PDRY still exists but the vital supply route into Dhofar is firmly held by SAF. There is a minor internal security problem, but the war is certainly over for the foreseeable future. It is surprising how few people know about the part played by British soldiers in securing peace and prosperity for this stategically important Arab state.

14

Conclusions

The conditions under which Britain's post-war campaigns were fought were predominantly rural, varying from jungle conditions (Malaya, Kenya, Borneo, Belize, Guyana, Dhofar) to desert conditions (Palestine, Muscat and Oman, Radfan, Kuwait). Some of the rural campaigns had an urban component (Palestine, Aden, Kenya) while two were predominantly urban counter-terrorist campaigns (Cyprus, Northern Ireland). The most striking feature of these campaigns is the degree of success achieved by the British Army in these medium and small-scale operations. In Malaya, Muscat and Oman, Borneo and Dhofar the enemy were militarily and politically defeated; in Kuwait and Guyana the timely deployment of military force avoided serious conflict and encouraged political developments that were by and large favourable to Great Britain; in Belize the same technique appears to have been equally successful to date; in Kenya the guerillas were virtually crushed and in Cyprus contained before political agreement in both cases was reached with Britain; Palestine and Aden cannot be judged political or military successes but certainly the Army came out of both campaigns rather better than anyone else; Northern Ireland of course remains unresolved but by most measures of success the Army can be said to have succeeded in a near impossible situation.

The political outcome of British Army activity was equally favourable to Great Britain. In virtually every case newly independent states allowed the British Army to retain facilities in their countries. Even in Palestine the forces that had fought Britain and subsequently set up the State of Israel, only eight years later joined with Britain and France in a military campaign against Nasser's Egypt. Only really in Aden did a guerilla movement challenge the terms of decolonization and subsequently support other guerillas against the British Army in Dhofar.

What conclusions can be drawn from this success? It is worth looking first at the military techniques or tactics employed. Perhaps most importantly the British Army has always been willing to play the terrorist at his own game. In Malaya and Borneo for instance the British fought the Communist terrorists not with artillery and air power but by inserting small patrols armed in much the same way as the men they were seeking. The tactics that they used employed stealth, patience and cunning. On the few occasions that artillery or bombers were used they were remarkably unsuccessful. Often such tactics have been more from necessity than by design. In both Malaya and Borneo and indeed in the Radfan and Dhofar it was usually the shortage of helicopters that forced commanders to seek an option more suited to the terrain rather than go for the easy solution of insertion by helicopter. Conversely it can be argued that the relatively generous holdings of helicopter assets by the Americans in Vietnam contributed to their military failure in that campaign. Whether or not this is true, it is a fact that the British Army has achieved a considerble measure of success in many of its campaigns by the use of straightforward infantry tactics without he same degree of artillery, engineer, air or other support. Indeed artillerymen and other branches of the army have often found themselves employed as infantrymen – much to their chagrin!

This 'infantry' approach to terrorist threats has gone hand-in-glove with the dictum of 'minimum force'. It has always been a basic tenet of British Army policy since 1945 that a given situation be met with the minimum degree of force required to solve it. In Georgetown, Guyana, in 1961 the situation did not get out of hand because the troops did not over-react. In Aden in 1967 General Tower did not re-occupy Crater immediately as it would have required considerable force to do so successfully including probably the 76-mm guns of the Saladin Armoured Cars. Instead he waited and the Argylls chose their moment to re-enter Crater stealthily and virtually without opposition. In Northern Ireland the 'No Go' areas in Londonderry and Belfast could have been stormed immediately using maximum force but again the right moment was chosen and they were re-occupied quietly after a period of occupation by the IRA. Such a policy cannot be popular with men who are trained to find quick and efficient solutions to military problems; it says a great deal for the British Army that it carries out a policy that is often militarily inefficient but politically expedient without complaint. The limitations imposed upon soldiers in Northern Ireland by the Yellow Card which lays down very strict circumstances when a soldier can open fire make life very difficult for him. It usually means that he cannot open fire unless fired upon. This is as it should be; however the enormous restraint shown by British soldiers in these difficult circumstances should not be taken for granted. Such restraint can only be achieved by disciplined, highly motivated and well trained soldiers.

Helicopters have provided tactical mobility for the army in most campaigns since the Malayan emergency. However, there has always been such a shortage of this asset that their use has not been a war-winning factor. Perhaps for the first time in Northern Ireland the army has roughly the number of helicopters that it can usefully employ. However in Muscat and Oman in 1957–59, in the Radfan in 1964 and Dhofar in 1970–76 fighter ground-attack aircraft played a prominent role in operations. On several occasions in the Radfan RAF aircraft rocketed dissident tribesmen within yards of British troops. The classic example of fighter aircraft saving the day was at Marbat during the Dhofar campaign when the arrival of the Strikemasters almost certainly prevented the SAS position being over-run.

Communication barriers have proved to be a most useful tool. Not to be confused with villagization or food control, of which more later, communication barriers were used with great success in both Kenya and Dhofar. In Kenya strips were cleared along the forest edges which were designed to make it more difficult for Mau Mau gangs to leave the forest undetected. In Dhofar the Damavand and Hornbeam Lines were physical barriers of barbed wire with Unattended Ground Sensors (UGS) at specific points and platoons of troops at regular intervals. Both the French in Algeria and the Americans in Vietnam had built communication barriers though neither with much success. In Dhofar barriers and UGS were successful mainly because the area through which the guerillas had to move their supplies was limited and predictable.

But military technique and expertise can only provide part of the answer to the British Army's success. Senior British officers have been fortunate in the co-operation they have always received from the civil administration. The decision for instance to run both the Malayan and Kenyan campaigns by means of District Security Committees involving the triumvirate of the army, the police and civilian representatives was both enlightened and effective. It allowed an agreed and workable policy to be put into effect. Military commanders learned what was practicable and civil servants what was possible. The main outcome was that each understood the other.

The decision to involve the local people in the fight against terrorism has always paid off: in Malaya and Kenya the home guard and the police, in the Radfan and Aden the FRA, in Dhofar the 'firqas', in Borneo the Iban trackers and the Dyaks and in Ulster the RUC and the UDR. This has often involved considerable political courage. For instance, the decision to arm the Kikuyu Home Guard was a brave one when it was from the Kikuyu that the Mau Mau drew its recruits. Usually a demonstration of trust has paid great dividends.

Villagization, food-control and the use of curfews and ID cards have been indispensable tools in the fight against terrorism. Though often unpopular and usually introduced as part of a wider package of emergency regulations, villagization has proved extremely effective particularly in Malaya and Kenya. The wholesale move of a village into new and unfamiliar surroundings can be construed as a harsh even cruel measure. But it was often the only way to isolate the terrorists and to prevent the intimidation of the population. Once settled in the new villages the people often found peace of mind. They were of course returned to their own villages after the emergency was ended.

Colonial authorities in many of Britain's Brush Fire Wars have conducted 'hearts and minds' campaigns in parallel with the military campaign. These were so called because they were designed to capture the hearts and minds of the people to support the government cause. Hearts and minds campaigns took different forms in different campaigns. In Malaya government teams provided expert advice on agricultural problems; in Borneo army doctors and medical orderlies visited kampongs providing medical aid and advice; again in Borneo and in Belize, British Guiana and Malaya helicopters evacuated civilian emergency medical cases to hospital; in Dhofar the Royal Engineers drilled water wells; in Muscat and Oman the villages on top of the Jebel Akhdar were provided with building materials via the new air strip; in Ulster helicopters have lifted stranded cattle from bogs while soldiers have organized facilities for underprivileged children. Though hearts and minds campaigns have been part and parcel of the overall plan to defeat terrorism, the enthusiasm with which they have been carried out has in most cases gone well beyond what is strictly required. From the unfortunate Jews aboard the *Exodus* in 1947 to the tortured people of Ulster in 1983 the British soldier has always shown a remarkable degree of understanding and tolerance.

Britain's Brush Fire Wars have generated a host of so-called 'Special Methods'. These inevitably have mainly been the province of the Intelligence Community. The incentives provided to disillusioned terrorists to change sides have been remarkably successful in several campaigns. In Malaya the Surrendered Enemy Personnel (SEP) numbered thousands; they were in large part responsible for leading many other waiverers out of the jungle to be rehabilitated into the community. In Kenya many disillusioned Mau Mau joined the pseudo-gangs which played such a vital part in the destruction of the Mau Mau. In Dhofar the Sultan's enemies were persuaded to defect in fairly large numbers. In Northern Ireland clearly much valuable intelligence is elicited from informers and 'supergrasses'.

The British have also proved to be masters of the co-ordination of their Intelligence assets. This has been largely due to the fact that they have been willing to include the local police and Special Branch in a co-ordinated intelligence organization. Military intelligence officers have been willing to live among the people, sometimes with no more than two or three assistants drawn from the local population in a small house sited away from a military base. In such a situation, though it was often dangerous, they were able to keep their ear to the ground. In Borneo, Field Intelligence Officers often knew of an Indonesian incursion within a very short time of its happening; their information came from villagers whose confidence they had won who reported anything suspicious over the field telephone system. Similar arrangements existed in Malaya and Kenya.

Particularly in the last ten years, and since the Northern Ireland campaign has been in progress, much special-purpose Internal Security (IS) equipment has been produced particularly in Great Britain and the United States. In a rural environment it has usually been possible to adapt conventional equipment to meet a terrorist threat but in an urban environment such as exists in Belfast or Londonderry it is both militarily sensible and politically expedient to develop or purchase special-purpose IS equipment. This includes water cannon, riot guns, rubber bullets, special armoured vehicles, bomb-detection and disposal equipment and much more. Some of this equipment is in use in Northern Ireland today and is contributing towards the defeat of terrorism there.

In these areas, then – in the tactics and techniques employed by the army, in the benign influence of the colonial administration upon the military and in the special methods and equipment developed by the army – lie most of the reasons for the extraordinary measure of success achieved by the British Army in brush fire warfare from 1945 to 1984. No other army has accumulated such a legacy of counter-terrorist experience and no other army has been so successful in the application of its experience. That the same expertise still abounds is evident in Northern Ireland and was dramatically demonstrated in May 1980 in the highly successful storming by the SAS of the Iranian Embassy in London. If any further evidence is needed the 1982 Falklands War provided it.

The Regiments are mostly home now. They have a wealth of memories and some stories to tell ...

Appendix A

Operational deployments of British Troops
1945-83

1945-48	Palestine (see chapter 2)
1947	Aden riots
1948	Gold Coast riots
	British Honduras (see chapter 4)
1948-60	Malaya (see chapter 3)
1948-51	Eritrea (operations against Shifta terrorists)
1950	Singapore (Hartog riots)
1950-53	Korean War
1951	Akaba (Moussadeq Oil Nationalization)
1952-56	Kenya (see chapter 5)
1953	British Guiana (see chapter 6)
1954-83	Cyprus (see chapter 7)
1955	Singapore riots
	Buraimi Oasis operations
1956	Bahrain riots
	Hong Kong riots
	Singapore riots
	Suez operations
1957	British Honduras (see chapter 4)
1957-59	Muscat and Oman (see chapter 8)
1958	Nassau strike
	Aden disturbances
	Jordan/Lebanon intervention
1959	Gan riots
1960	Jamaica (Rastafarian riots)
1960-61	Cameroons
1961	Kuwait (see chapter 9)
	Zanzibar
1962	British Honduras (see chapter 4)
	British Guiana (see chapter 6)
	Brunei (see chapter 10)
1963	Swaziland

	Zanzibar
1963-66	Borneo (see chapter 10)
1964	Zanzibar Revolution
	Tanganyika Army Mutiny
	Uganda Army Mutiny
	Kenya Army Mutiny
1964-67	Aden and Radfan (see chapter 11)
1965	Mauritius
	Bechuanaland
1966	Hong Kong riots
	Das Island
	Seychelles
1967	Hong Kong riots
1968	Bermuda State of Emergency
	Mauritius State of Emergency
1969	Anguilla
	Bermuda
1969-84	Northern Ireland (see chapter 12)
1970-76	Dhofar (see chapter 13)
1972	Bomb scare on *Queen Elizabeth 2* in mid-Atlantic and consequent para drop
1979-84	Rhodesia/Zimbabwe
1980	SAS assault on Iranian Embassy
	New Hebrides (Royal Marines)
1982	Falklands War
1983	Beirut

This list does not include flood, hurricane and earthquake relief, particularly by the Royal Engineers, in many countries throughout the world, and continuing operations in Hong Kong to prevent the flood of refugees from Communist China.

Appendix B

Organization of an Infantry Battalion, 1983

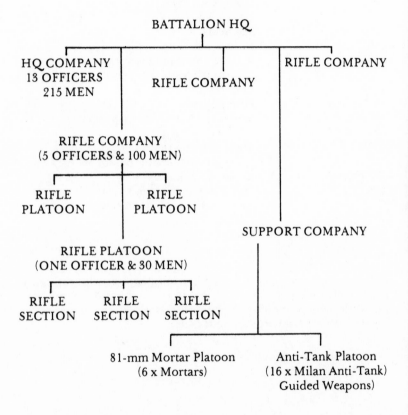

1. An Infantry Battalion is commanded by a Lieutenant-Colonel, a Company by a Major, a Platoon by a Lieutenant and a Section by a Corporal.

2. Battalion strengths have varied from 800 in 1945 to the current 650 in 1983.

3. Organizations have also varied. The organization shown has been the most widely used and still is.

4. Throughout most of the 1945-83 period the anti-tank platoon has been armed with direct fire recoiless rifles. The MILAN Guided weapon was issued in 1979.

5. HQ Company includes the Signals Platoon and the Motor Transport Platoon.

Appendix C

Regiments and Corps of the Regular Army 1949

Mounted Troops
The Life Guards *Also armoured*
Royal Horse Guards (The Blues) *Also armoured*
King's Troop, Royal Horse Artillery

Royal Armoured Corps
1st King's Dragoon Guards
The Queen's Bays (2nd Dragoon Guards)
3rd Carabiniers (Prince of Wales's Dragoon Guards)
4th/7th Royal Dragoon Guards
5th Royal Inniskilling Dragoon Guards
1st The Royal Dragoons
The Royal Scots Greys (2nd Dragoons)
3rd The King's Own Hussars
4th Queen's Own Hussars
7th Queen's Own Hussars
8th King's Royal Irish Hussars
9th Queen's Royal Lancers
10th Royal Hussars (Prince of Wales's Own)
11th Hussars (Prince Albert's Own)
12th Royal Lancers (Prince of Wales's)
13th/18th Royal Hussars (Queen Mary's Own)
14th/20th King's Hussars
15th/19th The King's Royal Hussars
16th/5th The Queen's Royal Lancers
17th/21st Lancers
Royal Tank Regiment *Eight regiments*

Supporting Arms
Royal Regiment of Artillery *Sixty-nine regiments*
Corps of Royal Engineers
Royal Corps of Signals

Foot Guards
Grenadier Guards *Three battalions*
Coldstream Guards *Three battalions*
Scots Guards *Two battalions*
Irish Guards
Welsh Guards

Infantry (Infantry Regiments consist of one battalion unless otherwise stated)
The Royal Scots (The Royal Regiment)
The Queen's Royal Regiment (West Surrey)
The Buffs (Royal East Kent Regiment)
The King's Own Royal Regiment (Lancaster)
The Royal Northumberland Fusiliers
The Royal Warwickshire Regiment
The Royal Fusiliers (City of London Regiment)
The King's Regiment (Liverpool)
The Royal Norfolk Regiment
The Royal Lincolnshire Regiment
The Devonshire Regiment
The Suffolk Regiment
The Somerset Light Infantry (Prince Albert's)
The West Yorkshire Regiment (The Prince of Wales's Own)
The East Yorkshire Regiment (The Duke of York's Own)
The Bedfordshire and Hertfordshire Regiment
The Royal Leicestershire Regiment
The Green Howards (Alexandra, Princess of Wales's Own Yorkshire Regiment)
The Lancashire Fusiliers
The Royal Scots Fusiliers
The Cheshire Regiment
The Royal Welch Fusiliers
The South Wales Borderers
The King's Own Scottish Borderers
The Cameronians (Scottish Rifles)
The Royal Inniskilling Fusiliers
The Gloucestershire Regiment
The Worcestershire Regiment
The East Lancashire Regiment
The East Surrey Regiment
The Duke of Cornwall's Light Infantry
The Duke of Wellington's Regiment (West Riding)
The Border Regiment
The Royal Sussex Regiment
The Royal Hampshire Regiment
The South Staffordshire Regiment

The Dorset Regiment
The South Lancashire Regiment (The Prince of Wales's Volunteers)
The Welch Regiment
The Black Watch (Royal Highland Regiment)
The Oxfordshire and Buckinghamshire Light Infantry
The Essex Regiment
The Sherwood Foresters (Nottinghamshire and Derbyshire Regiment)
The Loyal Regiment (North Lancashire)
The Northamptonshire Regiment
The Royal Berkshire Regiment (Princess Charlotte of Wales's)
The Queen's Own Royal West Kent Regiment
The King's Own Yorkshire Light Infantry
The King's Shropshire Light Infantry
The Middlesex Regiment (Duke of Cambridge's Own)
The King's Royal Rifle Corps
The Wiltshire Regiment (Duke of Edinburgh's)
The Manchester Regiment
The North Staffordshire Regiment (The Prince of Wales's)
The York and Lancaster Regiment
The Durham Light Infantry
The Highland Light Infantry (City of Glasgow Regiment)
Seaforth Highlanders (Ross-shire Buffs, The Duke of Albany's)
The Gordon Highlanders
The Queen's Own Cameron Highlanders
The Royal Ulster Rifles
The Royal Irish Fusiliers (Princess Victoria's)
The Argyll and Sutherland Highlanders (Princess Louise's)
The Rifle Brigade (Prince Consort's Own)
The Parachute Regiment *Three battalions and Guards company*

Army Air Corps
Glider Pilot Regiment *At cadre strength*
Special Air Service *No regular unit until 1950*

The Brigade of Gurkhas
2nd King Edward VII's Own Gurkha Rifles (The Sirmoor Rifles) *Two battalions*
6th Gurkha Rifles *Two battalions*
7th Gurkha Rifles *Two battalions*
10th Gurkha Rifles *Two battalions*
Gurkha Engineers

Services
Royal Army Chaplains' Department
Royal Army Service Corps

Royal Army Medical Corps
Royal Army Ordnance Corps
Corps of Royal Electrical and Mechanical Engineers
Corps of Royal Military Police
Royal Army Pay Corps
Royal Army Veterinary Corps
Small Arms School Corps
Military Provost Staff Corps
Royal Army Educational Corps
Royal Army Dental Corps
Royal Pioneer Corps
Intelligence Corps
Army Physical Training Corps
Army Catering Corps
General Service Corps
Queen Alexandra's Imperial Military Nursing Service
Queen Alexandra's Royal Army Nursing Corps
Women's Royal Army Corps

Regiments and Corps of the Regular Army as recognised in 1971

Mounted Troops
The Life Guards *Also armoured*
The Blues and Royals (Royal Horse Guards and 1st Dragoons) *Also armoured, formed 1969*
King's Troop, Royal Horse Artillery

Royal Armoured Corps
1st The Queen's Dragoon Guards *Formed 1959*
The Royal Scots Dragoon Guards (Carabiniers and Greys) *Formed 1971*
4th/7th Royal Dragoon Guards
5th Royal Inniskilling Dragoon Guards
The Queen's Own Hussars [3rd and 7th] *Formed 1959*
The Queen's Royal Irish Hussars [4th and 8th] *Formed 1958*
9th/12th Royal Lancers (Prince of Wales's) *Formed 1960*
The Royal Hussars (Prince of Wales's Own) [10th and 11th] *Formed 1969*
13th/18th Royal Hussars (Queen Mary's Own)
14th/20th King's Hussars
15th/19th The King's Royal Hussars
16th/5th The Queen's Royal Lancers
17th/21st Lancers
Royal Tank Regiment *Four regiments*

Parachute Squadron, Royal Armoured Corps *Formed 1964*

Supporting Arms
The Royal Regiment of Artillery *Twenty-nine regiments, three batteries*
The Corps of Royal Engineers
The Royal Corps of Signals

The Guards Division
Grenadier Guards *Two battalions*
Coldstream Guards *Two battalions*
Scots Guards
Irish Guards
Welsh Guards

The Scottish Division
The Royal Scots (The Royal Regiment)
The Royal Highland Fusiliers (Princess Margaret's Own Glasgow and Ayrshire Regiment) *Formed 1959*
The King's Own Scottish Borderers
The Black Watch (Royal Highland Regiment)
Queen's Own Highlanders (Seaforth and Camerons) *Formed 1961*
The Gordon Highlanders
The Argyll and Sutherland Highlanders (Princess Louise's) *reduced to company strength 1971 though later reconstituted to battalion strength*

The Queen's Division
The Queen's Regiment *Three battalions, one company Formed 1966*
The Royal Regiment of Fusiliers *Three battalions Formed 1968*
The Royal Anglian Regiment *Three battalions, one company Formed 1964*

The King's Division
The King's Own Royal Border Regiment *Formed 1959*
The King's Regiment *Formed 1958*
The Prince of Wales's Own Regiment of Yorkshire *Formed 1958*
The Green Howards
The Royal Irish Rangers *Two battalions. Formed 1968*
The Queen's Lancashire Regiment *Formed 1970*
The Duke of Wellington's Regiment (West Riding)

The Prince of Wales's Division
The Devonshire and Dorset Regiment *Formed 1958*
The Cheshire Regiment
The Royal Welch Fusiliers
The Royal Regiment of Wales *Formed 1969*
The Gloucestershire Regiment
The Worcestershire and Sherwood Foresters Regiment *Formed 1970*

The Royal Hampshire Regiment *Reduced to single company 1971 (later reconstituted to battalion strength)*
The Staffordshire Regiment (The Prince of Wales's) *Formed 1959*
The Duke of Edinburgh's Royal Regiment (Berkshire and Wiltshire) *Formed 1959*

The Light Division
The Light Infantry *Three battalions Formed 1968*
The Royal Green Jackers *Two battalions, one company (later reconstituted to battalion strength)*

Airborne
The Parachute Regiment *Three battalions, one Guards company*
22 Special Air Service Regiment
Army Air Corps *Reformed 1957*

The Brigade of Gurkhas
2nd King Edward VII's Own Gurkha Rifles (The Sirmoor Rifles) *Two battalions*
6th Queen Elizabeth's Own Gurkha Rifles *Renamed 1959*
7th Duke of Edinburgh's Own Gurkha Rifles *Renamed 1959*
10th Princess Mary's Own Gurkha Rifles *Renamed 1950*
Gurkha Engineers
Gurkha Signals
Gurkha Transport Regiment

Services
Royal Army Chaplains' Department
Royal Corps of Transport *Renamed 1965*
Royal Army Medical Corps
Royal Army Ordnance Corps
Corps of Royal Electrical and Mechanical Engineers
Corps of Royal Military Police
Royal Army Pay Corps
Royal Army Veterinary Corps
Small Arms School Corps
Military Provost Staff Corps
Royal Army Educational Corps
Royal Army Dental Corps
Royal Pioneer Corps
Intelligence Corps
Army Physical Training Corps
Army Catering Corps
General Service Corps
Queen Alexandra's Royal Army Nursing Corps
Women's Royal Army Corps

Appendix D

Infantry Battalions in the British Army, 1983

The Royal Scots (The Royal Regiment) *One battalion*
The Queen's Regiment *Three battalions*
The King's Own Royal Border Regiment *One battalion*
The Royal Regiment of Fusiliers *Three battalions*
The King's Regiment *One battalion*
The Royal Anglian Regiment *Three battalions*
The Devonshire and Dorset Regiment *One battalion*
The Light Infantry *Three battalions*
The Prince of Wales's Own Regiment of Yorkshire *One battalion*
The Green Howards (Alexandra, Princess of Wales's Own Yorkshire Regiment) *One battalion*
The Royal Highland Fusiliers (Princess Margaret's Own Glasgow and Ayrshire Regiment) *One battalion*
The Cheshire Regiment *One battalion*
The Royal Welch Fusiliers *One battalion*
The Royal Regiment of Wales (24th/41st Foot) *One battalion*
The King's Own Scottish Borderers *One battalion*
The Royal Irish Rangers (27th (Inniskilling) 83rd and 87th) *Two battalions*
The Gloucestershire Regiment *One battalion*
The Worcestershire and Sherwood Foresters Regiment (29th/45th Foot) *One battalion*
The Queen's Lancashire Regiment *One battalion*
The Duke of Wellington's Regiment (West Riding) *One battalion*
The Royal Hampshire Regiment *One battalion*
The Staffordshire Regiment (The Prince of Wales's) *One battalion*
The Black Watch (Royal Highland Regiment) *One battalion*
The Duke of Edinburgh's Royal Regiment (Berkshire and Wiltshire) *One battalion*
Queen's Own Highlanders (Seaforth and Camerons) *One battalion*
The Gordon Highlanders *One battalion*

The Argyll and Sutherland Highlanders (Princess Louise's) *One battalion*

The Parachute Regiment *Three battalions*

The Brigade of Gurkhas *Five battalions*

The Royal Green Jackets *Three battalions*

TOTAL: 47 Infantry Battalions

                     8 Guards Battalions (not included above)

GRAND TOTAL: 55 Battalions

Appendix E

British Army Casualties, 1945-84

Campaign	Killed	Wounded
Palestine	223	478
Malaya	509 (including 159 Gurkhas)	921 (incluc 308 Gurkh
British Honduras/Belize	Nil	Nil
Kenya	12	69
British Guiana	Nil	Nil
Cyprus	99	414
Muscat and Oman	6	6
Kuwait	Nil	Nil
Brunei and Borneo	75 (including 43 Gurkhas)	158 (incluc 87 Gurkh
Radfan and Aden	90	510
Northern Ireland (to 27 Jan 1984) not including UDR	371	Not knowr
Dhofar	24	55

Sources

1. *General*

Gregory Blaxland, *The Regiments Depart*, William Kimber 1971.
Anthony Varrier, *An Army for the Sixties*, Secker & Warburg 1966.
Frank Kitson, *Bunch of Fives*, Faber & Faber 1977.
Maurice Tugwell, *The Unquiet Peace*, Allan Wingate 1957.

2. *Palestine*

James Cameron, *The Making of Israel*, Secker and Warburg.
Noah Lucas, *The Modern History of Israel*, Weidenfeld and Nicolson.
David Ben Gurion, *Israel – A Personal History*, American–Israel Publishing Co.
John Marlowe, *Rebellion in Palestine*, Cresset Press 1946.
Menachim Begin, *The Revolt*, W.H. Allen 1951.

3. *Malaya*

Richard Miers, *Shoot to Kill*, Faber & Faber 1959
Richard Clutterbuck, *The Long Long War*, Cassell 1966.
Fred Majdalaney, *State of Emergency*, Longmans Green 1962.
Julian Paget, *Counter – Insurgency Campaigning*, Faber & Faber 1967.
J.B. Oldfield, *The Green Howards in Malaya*, Gale & Polden 1953.
Arthur Campbell, *Jungle Green*, Allen and Unwin 1953.
The Suffolk Regimental Gazette.
Mark Henniker, *Red Shadow over Malaya*, Blackwood 1955.
Discussions with Lt-Colonel Malcolm Dewar OBE, late of the Suffolk Regiment and a Company Commander in Malaya 1950-53.
Personal contacts by author in Malaya in 1966 and 1974.

4. *British Honduras/Belize*

Regimental Journal of the Royal Irish Rangers.
Notes on History of Belize, published by 2nd Battalion the Royal Irish Rangers 1979.

Regimental Journal of the 1st Battalion the Cheshire Regiment.
Soldier Magazine, 1980.
Discussions with Lt-Colonel Roger Wheeler, Commanding Officer of
the 2nd Battalion the Royal Irish Rangers in Belize in 1979.

5. *Kenya*

Frank Kitson, *Gangs and Counter Gangs*, Barrie and Rockliff 1960.
Counter Insurgency in Kenya 1952-60, Transafrica Publishers 1976.
Derwent Whittesey, *Kenya, the land and the Mau*, Foreign Affairs 1953.
Denis Holman, *Bwana Drum*, W.H. Allen 1964.
Donald L. Barnett and Karari Njama, *Mau Mau from within*,
McGibbon and Kee 1966.
Gerald Lathbury, *The Kenya Emergency 1955-56*, MOD paper 1958.
Numerous papers and manuscript recollections supplied by Colonel
Sir Guy Campbell, Commanding Officer of the Kenya Regiment
1952-56.

6. *British Guiana*

King's Royal Rifle Corps Chronicles.
Discussions with serving Green Jacket officers and NCOs who served
in British Guiana.
Discussions with my friend Martin Nascimento, now deceased, who
served in the Guyana Defence Force after Independence.
Ronald M. Schneider and Robert C. Kingsbury, *An Atlas of Latin
American Affairs*, Methuen 1966.

7. *Cyprus*

Nancy Crayshaw, *The Cyprus Revolt*, Allen & Unwin 1978.
Stanley Mayes, *Cyprus and Makarios*, Putnam and Co 1960.
Edited Foley, *Memoirs of General Grivas*, Clay & Co 1964.
D. Alastos, *Cyprus Guerilla*, Heinemann 1960.
Laurence Durrell, *Bitter Lemons*, Faber & Faber 1964
Regimental Chronicle of the Royal Green Jackets 1968 Edition.
Discussions with Lt-Colonel Malcolm Dewar, OBE, late of the
Suffolk Regiment and a Battalion Second-in-Command in Cyprus
1954–56.
Personal experiences in Cyprus in 1954–56, 1962–63, 1964 and 1970.
Regimental Chronicles of the Parachute Regiment.

8. *Muscat and Oman*

P.S. Allfree, *War Lords of Oman*, Robert Hale 1967.

Major K.W.D. Diane, *War in Oman*, Household Brigade Magazine 1959.

Colonel D. Smiley, *Muscat and Oman*, RUSI Journal 1960.

Brigadier A.J. Deane-Drummond, *Operation in Oman*, British Army Review 1959.

Major W.O. Little, *Oman Redivivus*, Army Quarterly 1956.

Operation in Muscat and Oman 1952–59, MOD 1964.

Material supplied by Major-General John Watts, CBE MC, now commander of the Sultan of Oman's Land Forces and in 1957–59 a squadron commander in the SAS in Oman.

9. *Kuwait*

Christine Osborne, *The Gulf States of Oman*, Croom Helm 1977.

A. Yodfat and M. Abir, *In the Direction of the Gulf*, Frank Cass 1977.

P. Mansfield, *The Middle East*, 5th Edition 1980.

Exchange of notes regarding relations between the United Kingdom and the State of Kuwait HMSO 1961.

Pegasus, Regimental Magazine of the Parachute Regiment, 1962 Edition.

R. Hewins, *Bush Fire*, Kuwait 1961.

John Marlowe, *The Persian Gulf in the 20th Century*, Cresset Press 1962.

10. *Brunei and Borneo*

Harold James and Denis Sheil-Small, *Undeclared War*, Leo Cooper 1971.

Observer Colour Magazine October 1964.

Malaysia – Indonesia Conflict, International Review Service 1965.

Regimental Chronicles of the Royal Green Jackets, Gurkhas, and the Royal Marines.

Personal experiences in Borneo as a Platoon Commander 1965–66.

Edgar O'Ballance, *Revolt in Borneo*, Article in Army Review July 1963.

Lt-General Sir Walter Walker, KCB, CBE, DSO, *How Borneo was Won*, The Round Table January 1969 Edition.

J.A.C. Mackie, *Konfrontasi*, Oxford University Press 1974.

Gisborne, *Naval Operations in the Malacca and Singapore Straits 1964–66*, Naval Review 1967.

Major-General J. Moulton, *A Brush Fire Operation – Brunei December 1962*, Brassey's Annual 1963.

11. *Radfan and Aden*

Julian Paget, *Last Post: Aden 1963–67*, Faber & Faber 1969.

Colin Mitchell, *Having Been a Soldier*, Hamish Hamilton 1969.

D.A. Schmidt, *Yemen*, Bodley Head 1968.

3rd Bn The Parachute Regiment in action in the Radfan, extract from *Pegasus* 1964.

Brigadier P. Shagland, *The Dhala Road*, Royal Engineers Journal 1969.

Major A.J. Stagg, *Gunners in the Radfan*, extract Journal of the Royal Artillery 1965.

Lt-Colonel T. Stevens, *Operations in the Radfan 1964*, RUSI Journal 1965.

Major J.E. Dent, *British soldier in Aden*, extract *Infantry* 1967.

12.   *Northern Ireland*

T.E. Utley, *Lessons of Ulster*, J.M. Dent & Sons 1976

D.P. Baritt and A. Booth, *Orange and Green*, Northern Friends Peace Board 1972.

Brian Maw Whinney and Ronald Wells, *Conflict and Christianity in Northern Ireland*, Lion Publishing 1975.

Conor Cruise O'Brien, *Hands Off*, Article in *Foreign Policy*, Winter 1979 –80 Edition.

Rawle Knox, *Ulster: Ireland's Blind Eye*, article in the Round Table October 1979.

David Barzilay, *The British Army in Ulster Vols I, II and III*, Century Books Vol. I 1973, Vo. II 1975 Vol. III 1978.

Regimental Chronicles of the Royal Green Jackets, the Parachute Regiment and the Light Infantry.

Discussions with Lt-Colonel Peter Treneer-Michel OBE, Battalion Commander in Ulster 1979.

Personal experiences in Ulster as a Company Commander in Belfast 1974.

Various IRA and UDA broadsheets.

The Compton Report, HMSO 1971.

Martin Wallace *Northern Ireland, 50 years of self government*, David & Charles 1971.

Tony Gray, *Psalms and Slaughter, a Study in Bigotry*, William Heinemann Ltd 1972

James Callaghan, *A House Divided*, William Collins 1973.

13.   *Dhofar*

Tony Geraghty, *Who Dares Wins*, Arms and Armour Press 1980.

Material supplied by Major-General John Watts (see Muscat and Oman Sources).

Papers and scripts supplied by Major-General John Akehurst.

Material supplied by various serving SAS Officers (security prevents me from divulging their names).

R. Fiennes, *Where British Soldiers Still Die Under a Foreign Flag*, *Observer Magazine* 1971.

John Townsend, *Oman, The Making of a Modern State*, Croom Helm 1977.

Index of British Formations and Units

Index